HEARING

US

OUT

Voices from the Gay and Lesbian Community

BY ROGER SUTTON

WITH A FOREWORD BY M.E. KERR

Photographs by Lisa Ebright

Hearing Us Out

HEARING US OUT

Voices from the Gay and Lesbian Community

BY ROGER SUTTON

WITH A FOREWORD BY M. E. KERR

Photographs by Lisa Ebright

Little, Brown and Company
Boston New York Toronto London

For Richard, Ruth, and Ruth
R. S.

For Michael
L. E.

Text copyright © 1994 by Roger Sutton
Foreword copyright © 1994 by M. E. Kerr
Photographs copyright © 1994 by Lisa Ebright

First Paperback Edition
Library of Congress Cataloging-in-Publication Data
Sutton, Roger.
    Hearing us out : voices from the gay and lesbian community / by Roger
Sutton ; photographs by Lisa Ebright ; with a foreword by M. E. Kerr. —
1st ed.
        p.   cm.
    ISBN 0-316-82326-0 (hc)   ISBN 0-316-82313-9 (pb)
1. Gays — United States — Identity.   2. Gays — United States —
Interviews.   3. Coming out (Sexual orientation)
[1. Homosexuality.   2. Gays — Interviews.   3. Lesbians — Interviews.]
I. Ebright, Lisa, ill.   II. Title.
HQ76.3.U5S88   1994
305.9´0664—dc20   94-20206

10 9 8 7 6 5 4 3 2 1
MAR
Printed simultaneously in Canada by Little, Brown & Company (Canada) Limited
Printed in the United States of America

ACKNOWLEDGMENTS

My first thanks go to the people I interviewed for this book, both the ones included and the ones who for various reasons had to be omitted. I've never heard such an assortment of brave, honest, and funny stories. Thanks are also due to everybody who helped me find interview subjects.

I would like to thank all my collaborators: Lisa Ebright, for her terrific pictures; Ann Rider, for her smart questions and sharp editing; Betsy Hearne, for rousing me from my habitual laziness and for her sensitive reading of the manuscript; and Deborah Stevenson, who transcribed all the interviews and provided me with many astute and subtle observations.

Two long-time friends and colleagues, Hazel Rochman and Elizabeth Law, listened and listened some more while I got this book written.

Ruth Saks and Ruth Ketchum were among the first gay people I ever met (and loved); years of debate with them continue to build my understanding of what community means.

Richard Asch put up with *a lot* during the three years this book consumed my attention, as well as giving me much practical assistance. Thanks, sweetie.

— *Roger Sutton*

Thank you to all the people in this book who welcomed my camera into their lives, and a special thank-you to Roger Sutton for asking me to participate in a creative and important project. I also appreciate all the artistic and editorial help from Susan Lu and Ann Rider of Little, Brown and Company.

Kudos to Linda for patience, laughter, and the trip to Madison.

— *Lisa Ebright*

CONTENTS

FOREWORD

A psychologist, who was also the mother of a dwarf, traveled to my home in the Hamptons to try and discover how I had come to write my book *Little Little,* which is about a teenage dwarf.

"How do you know so much about the denial and intragroup prejudice and the rest?"

I told her that growing up homosexual in the late '30s and early '40s had given me all my insights.

I had always been haunted by the story of this rich and beautiful young couple in a nearby small town, whose first child was a dwarf. But I had never found the "voice" for the main character, until one night I realized it was my own voice.

At our weekly consciousness-raising group, sponsored by the East End Gay Organization (EEGO), I listened to a young architect tell of being kicked out of prep school after being caught in another boy's room after light bell. He was ready, by then, to confess his homosexuality to his parents, but they insisted it was just a stage and sent him for boxing lessons.

All of us in the group whose parents "found out" in various ways that we were gay were told it would pass, or it could be corrected. We were sent to doctors, ministers, rabbis (and in my case, ballet class) to see if it wouldn't just disappear by the wisdom of a psychologist, the power of prayer, the grace of a *pas de chat.*

The parents of the dwarf had put their child through similar "cures": exercise, prayers, hormones. . . . And then they told themselves she is short, yes, but not *that* short . . . the same as many of our parents who finally could divine the truth of our attraction to the same sex, then insisted we were *bisexual*—succotash, yes, but not straight beans!

In our EEGO group we talked, too, about how very early into our own self-acceptance, we could not yet tolerate those among us who "looked it." I remember one of the first appearances of male and female homosexuals on an afternoon TV talk show in the 1970s. We sat waiting for it to begin, holding our breath and hoping the men wouldn't be too nance, the women too butch. It took a while to grasp the meaning of gay pride, and that it did not mean looking and acting as straight as possible.

The dwarf who'd been the inspiration for my book joined Little People of America so she would know others like her, but kept a list of the *p.f.'s*, who were "perfectly formed" as she was, not wanting to hang out with the ones with humps or twisted legs.

The vast majority of us (dwarfs and gays) grew up without a peer group, and with parents who had no familiarity with the subject. I can remember my mother, when I was home one summer on vacation from boarding school, grabbing my arm suddenly at the country club, stopping us in our tracks to whisper, "Look, Marijane, there's Ellie Poole down the lawn with that woman! You know she's left her husband, did I write you? She's become a fairy."

When my mother finally did come to terms with me and with terms ("I hate that word *lesbian* and I'll never call you one!"), she asked that there be one promise: "Never bring any of them to this house! . . . And stay in New York City where anything goes, because around here I couldn't hold my head up if it ever got out."

As I read *Hearing Us Out: Voices from the Gay and Lesbian Community*, I thought of what this book might have meant not just to someone like me, growing up gay, but also to a parent like my mother, who was not that different from many of her time. If only there had been literature for her to read, besides the heavy and pathetic *Well of Loneliness*. If only she had some confirmation that this blight on our family was not as rare and terrible as she believed it was. My father could not even speak about it.

So formed by what others thought, so in thrall to convention and conformity, both my parents missed the chance to know my warm and loving friends—as well as to know me better.

I feel sorry for all the people who miss the chance to know us. One of my great blessings is being part of this community that refuses to be diminished by the prejudice or rigidity of others. Despite it all, too, we've learned how to love and have fun and be family.

Listen to our many voices.

— *M. E. Kerr*
Author of Night Kites *and*
Deliver Us from Evie

INTRODUCTION

When I was in high school, twenty years ago, there were no books about homosexuality written for teenagers. There were certainly no books about the gay community. There were a couple of young adult novels that bravely, if gingerly, began to explore the theme, but I wasn't aware of them then, and my reading material on the subject was limited to one or two chapters in Dr. David Reuben's *Everything You Always Wanted to Know About Sex but Were Afraid to Ask,* a huge best-seller of the early '70s and a copy of which my mother had stashed in the right-hand drawer of her bureau, underneath a pile of socks that I (and my three brothers, I was to learn later) easily moved aside.

Reuben's book is pretty scary when it comes to homosexuality. I recall one graphic depiction of a gay "date" that consisted of anonymous sex in someone's front hall; another memorable statement was Reuben's take on lesbianism: "One vagina plus another vagina equals zero."

Like the teenagers interviewed in this book, I had feelings, crushes, fantasies — times of denial and other times of looking into a mirror and whispering, "You are gay." Unlike them, however, it would never have occurred to me to go to a gay teen group. I had never heard of such a thing, and if I had, I still wouldn't have gone. It was simply too scary.

It was not until college that I told anyone I thought I was gay. I was three thousand miles away from home, and in a much more "alternative" atmosphere. There was a gay students union, and they held dances. There was a sociology class called "Stigmatized Sexual Behavior," which, it was rumored, all the gay people took. Although I had gay and lesbian friends, they were still *them.* I stayed away from both the dances and the class until the second half of my sophomore year, when I told my best friend, Ruth, who was intense, frank, and witty about her own lesbianism, that I thought I *might* be gay. I still hadn't done anything about it, but I was facing the fact that my sexual and romantic feelings were toward men.

I soon was going to meetings of the Gay Students Union, which was my first experience with a gay community. As I've learned ever since, my community is bigger than where I live. It includes gay and lesbian people I know around the world, but it also includes people I've never met, such as gay writers or pop stars or politicians. It even includes people I've never heard of, like the fifteen-year-old lesbian who's afraid to check this book out of her school library. It includes straight people — there are some in this book, and every year, the group that gets the most heartfelt cheers at gay pride parades is P-FLAG, Parents, Families and Friends of Lesbians and Gays.

Most important, a community includes ideas: shared beliefs and shared arenas of disagreement. The reason we talk about the gay community, or the gay and lesbian community (more on this later), instead of the homosexual community, is that *homosexual* simply describes a psychological set of attitudes and behaviors, whereas *gay* describes a culture, one that I wanted to explore in this book. I like being around other gay people. I seek them out because I want friends — and allies — "like me." Each of us has many different "like me's": the other people on the track team can be "like me"; at the same time, others who share my religion are "like me." With each group you share common goals, vocabulary, tradition, and jokes, some of which won't mean much to the uninitiated. (What does a lesbian bring on a second date? A moving van. Get it?) I read recently in the *New York Times* that the deaf were the only American culture not united by family background: most deaf people are born to hearing parents. Well, it wasn't my mother who taught me to love opera.

That's another thing. Stereotypes. Most nonfiction published for young adults about gayness gets very stern on the subject of stereotypes. Don't exist, they say. Straight people like opera, too. Gay people are just like everybody else; they "just happen" to "prefer" sexual relations with their own sex. That's all that's different. That point of view is well meaning but unintentionally *de*meaning, because it takes away from gay people their history, stories, and — most politically damaging — their sense of themselves as a group. Take AIDS, for example. We all know how that disease has killed many gay men, along with others. To say "It has nothing to do with being gay — AIDS can strike anybody" is true, but, again I think unintentionally, dismissive of the centrality of AIDS to the gay experience and of the incredible responses — medical, political, financial, spiritual, and artistic — that that community has made to the disease. AIDS has not only changed sexual practices among gay men, it has changed what being gay means, and its effects will be felt long after the disease has been eradicated or run its course.

One thing communities do is name themselves. Lots of names have floated through the gay community. *Homophile, friend of Dorothy's,* and *Sapphic* are some gems from the past; right now there's something of a vogue for *queer.* That's a name employed by both gay men and lesbians, and its use, these days, usually implies a more confrontational stance of defiance. Of course, a lot depends on who's saying it: Compare "I'm queer" to "You're queer" to "*You* queer."

I had to explain to my editor, who is smart, tough, and careful — but straight — why the subtitle of this book had to be "Voices from the Gay and Lesbian Community," rather than "Voices from the Gay Community." Some lesbians by whom I ran the title said it had to read "Voices from the Lesbian and Gay Community," but although I understand their point, I maintain that the first is easier to say, and therefore preferable. Try it. But there *is* the point: lesbians today are coming from two, sometimes but not always different strands of social change — feminism and gay liberation — and so their politics, social concerns, and culture will often take them in another direction. Even today, when the cultural gap — so wide for so long — between gay men and lesbians is narrowing and even closing here and there, we still have different magazines, political goals, and favorite singers (although k. d. lang does seem to win hearts all around). Is AIDS a lesbian issue? Does pro-gay mean pro-choice? The arguments continue, and there has to be room for both of us in "The name." Yvonne Zipter talks about some of these issues in chapter 5; Art Johnston, interviewed in chapter 9, was so careful when talking to me to always use "gay-and-lesbian" that he at one point ran away with himself and talked about what it was like when he was "a young gay and lesbian." With all due respect to both, I have in my introductory notes in this book sometimes abbreviated the phrase to "gay community" in the interests of brevity.

I'd like to say a bit about how subjects were chosen and interviewed for this book. While the primary audience intended here is young adults — gay, straight, bisexual, or still-thinking-about-it — the editor and I decided from the beginning that we would speak with both teens and adults, with more of the latter. There are other good books where gay teens speak (see the reading list at the back of the book), but I wanted a book that would show a greater range of experience, from a fifteen-year-old (chapter 10) to a grandmother (chapter 12), and include people who are living through some of the headline issues facing the gay and lesbian community today: AIDS, the military, gay parenting, and an actively hostile adversary in the religious right. I also thought it was important to show teenage gays and lesbians in particular that life goes on past junior-high humiliation and high-school ostracism. Jeff Rivera, in chapter 1, speaks forcefully and funnily about peer-group harassment; Terrence Smith, in chapter 4, shows that you can get beyond it. There is hope — which is also why I thought it was important to include photographs where possible. When you feel like you're "the only one," as so many gay kids do, it helps to see the faces of others "like you."

Calculation, serendipity, and community each played a part in finding subjects for this book. Yvonne Zipter knew Dorothy Knudson. I met Renee Hanover while lighting her cigarette at a benefit. My colleague Deborah Stevenson knew someone who knew Ed Kassing. Jeri Lynn Fields introduced me to several teens in the youth groups she coordinates. I conducted all but one of the interviews face-to-face, tape-recorded the conversation, and edited each transcript into a first-person narrative. This included trimming, culling, moving sentences around for clarity, and occasionally, having a question of mine put into the respondent's mouth in order to remind readers what we're talking about. (I also eliminated redundancies, especially after my transcriber grumbled, "I'm sick to death of typing the word *supportive*.")

Nobody knows how many gay people there are. Nobody, for that matter, has been able to definitively figure out exactly what a gay person is. Is it defined by who you have sex with? Who you *want* to have sex with? Do you have to "try" a heterosexual relationship before you can know for sure? What if you've been involved with both men and women? I spent last New Year's Eve with my boyfriend and three other couples. Two gay couples, two lesbian couples. None of the couples knew all of the other couples well, and a getting-to-know-you after-dinner conversation began with the seemingly casual question, "So, how did you two meet?" From that evolved another inevitable question, "How did you know you were gay?" There were three ex-spouses, seven children, one impending grandchild, and eight different stories among us. Some people knew in high school, or college. Another, at the age of forty and divorced, fell in love with her best friend, a woman. One of the men, a college professor, was asked out by one of his former students, and here they were at the New Year's table, seventeen years later. Takes all kinds.

In the twenty years since I first began looking for them, there have been at least a couple of dozen books on homosexuality published for teenagers and young adults. Most of these, some of them excellent choices, have been novels. But much of the nonfiction I've seen is either directed toward straight readers (and all those references to "them" can really get on a gay person's nerves) or is strictly psychological or health-related, with little discussion of gays and lesbians as a group, united in history, culture, political goals, and perpetual disagreement. The people in this book each have a different story to tell, but in some ways the stories add up and answer the same question: "What does being gay or lesbian mean to you?" Ask yourself the same question. Maybe it will be a question about a parent, or a sister, or a friend. Maybe it will be about people you see on TV or read about in the newspaper. Maybe it will be a question about you.

HEARING US OUT

"My school counselors said, 'Turn straight and you won't be harassed.'"

CHAPTER ONE

JEFF RIVERA

Is there ever a right time, a right place, a right way, to come out as a gay person? The phrase "coming out" is an old one, a campy takeoff on debutante-speak, but the experience itself is generally anything but lighthearted. While parental response to the news that a child is homosexual can run the gamut from rejection to acceptance (or often the one intertwined with the other), the moms or dads who are genuinely happy about the revelation are few. Reactions from friends can run along the same lines, and if it becomes general knowledge — or even suspected — at school, you run the very real risk of being harassed and beaten up. Telling an employer (as other interviews in this book discuss) can get you fired. Telling the army (as Ed Kassing discusses in chapter 6) can get you kicked out. But for Jeff, and for increasing numbers of other gay people, it's too frustrating to live with the secret.

I was around fourteen when I started having all these feelings and things, but by the time I was fifteen, I started wanting to find out more. I had a friend go to the library and take out a book, *When Someone You Know Is Gay*, because I was too nervous to take it out for myself. I didn't want them to think I was gay, you know? I read it over and over again. It helped knowing that there were other gay youth, from all kinds of backgrounds, who were feeling the same way I was. I had thought if you're gay, you're either not Catholic or you come from a broken family. I'm Catholic, and not in a broken family. So then I thought, I can't be gay. I don't want to wear a dress, I don't like lipstick. I'm just not gay. Someone's putting this into my mind or something. The devil, maybe. I was praying, "Please, God, make me not be gay. Please, God, make these feelings go away." I would pray all night and sit there crying and crying, "Oh, I can't be gay." I'd go to church every Sunday hoping I would change. But nothing worked.

So I talked to my best friend, Norma. We worked together at a video store, and we were really close, so I just said, "I think I'm gay." She said, "No, you're not gay. I'll take you to the church, I'll take you to the psychiatrist, you're just sick in the head." But I had read so much that I knew exactly what to say and I was prepared. She said, "No, someone made you gay." "No, nobody made me gay." "You were raped, weren't you, by a priest. You were molested by a priest. Tell me you were molested by a priest." "No, I wasn't." "You saw someone that was gay." "No, I didn't. I don't know nobody that's gay." "Someone touched you in a bad way." "No, nobody touched me — nothing!"

We argued for two weeks. Customers would be coming into the video store, and I would be there yelling at Norma, "No, no, *no*! Not this and that, and . . ." It was just like a battle. We're both real stubborn anyway, always seeing who's number one and who's right. Finally she said — I don't know how, but she accepted it — she said okay. She became one of the coolest persons on earth. She goes to the gay parade every year, and she gets very upset if someone says something like "fag."

Norma was the person who told my parents I was gay. I asked her to. I couldn't do it myself. When I came out to Norma, I said, "Now, I'm never going to come out to my parents until I die." But it's just one of those things I had in me for such a long time, so that when I told her, it felt so good inside, it was like a feeling of — *ahhhh*. It just clicked, and I told her, "You tell my parents now — do it now." She's very close to my family. We were at work, and my family lived upstairs from where I worked, so I said, "Go tell 'em now." I called my mom, and I told her, "Mom, my friend Norma is going to tell you something, and I hope you still love me." My mom started crying, "What? What are you going to tell us? Don't tell me you're going to get married to her! Please, tell me you're not going to get married." I said, "No, Mom, no. It's not that." "Don't tell me you're on drugs — please, don't tell me you're on drugs." "No, Mom." "Don't tell me you're in a gang — don't tell me you're going to get killed." I said, "No, Mom. Please tell me you still love me." She said, "Okay, I love you no matter what."

So Norma went upstairs and came back down about an hour later, and she didn't say nothing. I'm like, "Tell me, tell me, what, *what?*"

And she's saying, "Hold on, let me take care of the customers." "No, tell me! Tell me! Have they kicked me out of the house already?" And she says, "No, no, they didn't do nothing like that — they still love you." So then my mom calls me, and she says, "I still love you no matter what — I don't care." I said, "Okay, everything's fine," but when I got upstairs and went into my bedroom, there's a Bible on my bed. I said, "Mom, what does this have to do with me being gay?" And she says, "No, it's just someone put this in your brain, right?" So here we go all over again. "The priest, right? You have to go to a priest, right?" "No, mom, I don't want to go to no priest." "Someone did something. Someone molested you, right? Right?" "No, nobody did nothing." "Please, this isn't true. You're just confused — you're only fifteen. You just haven't gone out with the perfect girl. You haven't found the right woman." My dad was just sitting there; he wasn't saying nothing. He wouldn't even get into it. He was like, "Okay, I don't care." My mom was the one saying, "Oh, I'm not going to have grandkids. What am I going to tell the neighbors? Oh, God, the neighbor next door, she's going to know you're gay. Oh, God, she's never going to talk to me again. Oh, God, what am I going to do? Don't tell nobody! The family! Oh, my God. They're never going to talk to us. What about the grandkids!"

I kept on saying, "Mom, I want to have kids." She says, "You can't have kids if you're gay." "Yes, I can, Mom — I'll adopt." And she says, "No, you'll turn them gay, too." "Mom, here, read this book," and I gave her several books, and she read them, and she still said, "I have to take you to a psychiatrist," so she called the psychiatrist and said, "Please, my son's gay — hurry, do something, make him change."

So I went to the psychiatrist with my mom and my dad, and my mom says, "He's gay, make him change, he's wrong, he can't be gay." And the psychiatrist says, "No, lady, *you're* wrong." The psychiatrist just said no, flat out. "He's the way he is and nobody did nothing and he's gay and it's not because something happened to him." My mom still wouldn't accept it: "I'm taking him to another psychiatrist — I'll go to another psychiatrist." And the psychiatrist told my mom, "Take him to whatever psychiatrist you want — they'll all say the same." So we stayed, and we went every week to talk about how we were dealing with it. My dad took it pretty easily — me and him never talk, so it was, like, no big deal. He didn't say nothing bad; he didn't say nothing good. But he accepted it, he talked about it. My mom was the one that was all off the wall. It was three months of torture. But she finally got over it.

She finally even drove me to a gay youth group meeting. I had still not met anyone else gay at that point. My mom took me on a Saturday, when they had a drop-in group, and I didn't want to go in. I said, "No, there's going to be guys in dresses — they're going to have lipstick, and I'm going to feel *stupid*. I'm going to be the only one without a dress! No, Mom, I don't want to go in! They're going to be all weird in leather, Mom! They're going to take advantage of me!" But my mom said, "Come on, come on, you have to go in, come on."

When I went in there, I was like, "Wow! That guy looks straight, just like me!" It was pretty easy. You just meet other people, talk about your problems. It was nice.

School was different. My mom knew I was gay, my best friend knew I was gay, so it was hard to go to school and not tell anyone. I had just started high school and was trying to deal with *how* I was going to come out at school or *if* I was going to come out at school or what I was going to do. Everyone thought I was straight. I told one friend there that I was gay and she told someone else, and I went out for lunch and when I came back to school, I think half of the school knew. Everyone was staring at me weird, so I was thinking, Oh, God, don't tell me what I think happened, happened. A lot of people starting saying things to me. It was hard, real hard. People said, "Oh, you fag, I'm going to beat you up after school." And I didn't know what to do. I would go tell the teacher; the teacher wouldn't know what to do. He could stop it in his class, but that's it.

I couldn't go to my locker without being afraid of finding a note saying, "We're going to kill you, fag," and finally I said, "I'm going to tell the person in charge of discipline." He wasn't there, so they told me to go to my counselor. So I told my counselor I'm gay and I'm being harassed, and he just stared at me and said, "Are you sure you're gay?" And I said, "Yeah, I'm gay, and I'm being harassed. Can you do something about it?" And he said, "You want us to do something about it?" I say, "Yeah, they're harassing me, they're putting notes on my locker, I can't study, I can't come to school, I can't walk to school without people doing things or saying things." He picks up the telephone and calls someone else, and now there's *two* people in there, and they're saying, "So, you're gay." I'm like, "Yes, I am! I just want someone to stop them harassing me! Do something!" "Well, we really can't do nothing about it. Just don't tell nobody you're gay. Okay? Just tell them you're not gay, and it will stop." And I said, "No, I don't want to hide it. I should be able to tell people I'm gay and do what I want as long as I'm studying and coming to school and not being a problem." They said, "Well, if you find that you want to tell people you're gay, then we can't do nothing about it, really." So I said, "Fine, I'm calling my mom and dad right now." "You're calling *who*, young man?" "My mom and dad. Because you won't do anything about it. I'm going to tell them." Then they kind of got nervous and said, "Well, tell us who was harassing you."

Nothing changed. It got to a point that I wouldn't even leave for lunch anymore. Gym was painful, too. My grade in gym went from an A to an F because I wouldn't change my clothes because I didn't want to go to the locker room to get harassed. It got so bad that I just started not going to gym. Then the other classes got so bad, I just started calling in sick. "Mom, I'm sick." I would start making excuses with my mom. "Mom, I'm sick, I can't go to school, Mom, I'm sick." It was true torture, people would call me fag and leave things on my locker. I couldn't even eat in the lunchroom because food was thrown at me. It was hard, so I couldn't take it. My grades all went down, and they kicked me out of school.

They sent me to this alternative school for dropouts and said if my grades got better, they would let me back in. I love school, so I said, "Okay, we'll give it a try." I went to that alternative school. I found that it was worse than regular school because most people there were in gangs. So I dropped out of that. I just didn't go. They didn't kick me out; I dropped out because it was worse. It wasn't in a very good neighborhood, and the teachers didn't do anything. I went back to my old

Jeff in front of his former school

school to talk with the new principal, but she wouldn't let me back in. I get so mad when I think about it. They said it was my fault because I should have come to school. But I said, "I can't come to school when I'm being harassed and can't study, so what's the point?" I would sit there in school and I would try to read and they would throw paper at me and call me a fag. I would tell the teacher, and the teacher would say, "Well, just move over there. Move over there." finally there were teachers who wouldn't even do anything, just look at me ugly like "Well?" Like saying, "You want to be gay? Well, turn straight and you wouldn't have this problem."

I couldn't believe the teachers. Back then there was only one teacher I knew who really cared. You'd think that teachers would understand. They were sometimes worse than the students. I thought, They're teachers; they should be more tolerant. They know more. They were worse. They knew I was gay, and they'd sit there saying, "Oh, he's homosexual — they're trying to take over the planet." In Massachusetts, they made a law that you can't discriminate against any gay or lesbian youths in public schools. I wish there was something like that here. I think I would have still been in school.

Right now I'm working, but I want to get my GED, then go to college. This school really pissed me off — the teachers pissed me off — so now I'm like, "I'll show you all, teachers — just wait."

I guess my school is different now. It's just been two years, but now there are openly gay people there, and there's more awareness. I see several gay kids that are out, and though it's just been two years since I left, it seems like more straight people are saying, "I don't care if you're gay." I had a lot of people who didn't like me back then, but when I went back to visit, some people would come up to me and say things like "I'm sorry for what I said. I didn't mean to hurt your feelings. I just found out my cousin's gay."

"Many of the young people who come here don't even think they're going to survive adolescence." —Jerri Lynn

JERRI LYNN FIELDS AND MICHAEL CORNICELLI

According to a survey reported by the National Gay and Lesbian Task Force, one in four gay teens is forced to leave home over conflicts with parents about sexual identity, some seeking to survive on the streets by prostitution or dealing drugs. While many others are in less desperate situations, most still feel a sense of alienation from their families and straight peers. Horizons, a primary provider of social services to Chicago's gay and lesbian community, is there to offer a place to listen. I asked Jerri Lynn Fields, coordinator of the youth discussion groups, and Michael Cornicelli, a volunteer in the program, to give an overview of the challenges gay, lesbian, and bisexual teens face and how Horizons is addressing those issues. Organizations like Horizons can be found in many cities; see the list of resources at the end of this book.

JERRI LYNN: When a young person makes the decision to come here, he or she has often felt very isolated. They think they're the only one in their high school who feels this way, and they're the only one in their church or in the neighborhood. As soon as they walk through the door, they're going to see thirty to fifty other youth who've felt the exact same thing. I think that at least one wall comes down when they see that, because it's like, "Finally — so maybe there are thirty other people like me in the world," and then they're going to find out later that there are lots more than that.

We have peer support groups for young adults, fourteen to twenty-three years old, who are either lesbian, gay, bisexual, or questioning their sexual orientation. I organize the groups, manage the grants and the funding; I do marketing and outreach. I spend a good deal of my time outside of the agency going into high-school classrooms, working with teachers and social workers so that youth who can't make it to Horizons will, hopefully, have sensitive youth service providers working with them. Last year we saw 540 kids, about 60 percent males, 40 percent young women.

When young adults come in here, it's confidential. We don't take any names. It's never written down that they've been here. We don't keep files; we can't even confirm that someone is coming here. So if a parent were to call, we can't confirm that. I do get phone calls from parents whose son or daughter has either said, "I'm going to Horizons" or they've found a pamphlet or brochure lying around the house. Most of those phone conversations turn out pretty positively. They may be angry at first, and they have questions, and while I would never say, "Yes, your son or daughter is coming here," I'll refer them to P-FLAG, Parents, Families and Friends of Lesbians and Gays, and that's it. We also have parents who call wanting to refer their son or daughter here and wanting more information about the program. Kids themselves hear about us through their friends, or through their teachers and their guidance counselors. We advertise in the gay and lesbian newspapers and magazines and in the Chicago public schools newspaper.

We have adult advisers here every night, and although they're busy organizing discussion groups or just keeping some kind of order, I think one of their most important functions is being role models — just being here and being alive and having a healthy life and feeling very comfortable with their sexual orientation. Many of the young people who come here don't even think they're going to survive adolescence. They have attempted suicide, or they're thinking about it, because they think death would be better than being gay or lesbian or bisexual. But when they walk in here, they'll see at least eight to ten very confident, healthy adults.

MICHAEL: Part of what we do here is to try and give the teens an appreciation of the context in which they're living now, what led up to it, what the struggles of people were twenty, thirty, forty, or more years ago. And what struggles people are still coping with. I mean, for youth coming into an agency like this in a big city, it's still a very different kind of environment from what someone would find even today back in the small town in Ohio where I grew up.

I'm a volunteer in the youth services group. I'm generally here on the evening set aside for the younger group, fourteen through twenty years old. I'm in the drop-in room upstairs to mix with them, answer their questions, and basically just be available for them. When the drop-in sessions are ended, we have small-group discussions on a wide range of topics. For example, we did a program on religion: what were your experiences with organized religion, how were you raised, what messages did you get from it, how did it make you feel, where do you think those attitudes came from, those sorts of things. Other topics have been dating, prejudices that are faced in the community, what you like and what you don't like about your lifestyle. Usually those groups start with some sort of an icebreaker, and then develop into a discussion of the issues involved.

The group is so diverse. If you can imagine a boy from a small town and somebody from the projects and somebody else from a wealthy suburb — and they're all here together. Sometimes that's difficult from the standpoint of programming, but I can't say that it's a problem among the youth. I've seen them be cruel, as all kids can be, but I have also seen them be remarkably supportive of someone with a problem. They'll be in a group discussion and someone will be relating a story about some awful thing that happened to them or someone who wronged them in some fashion, and I've seen the others gather around that person and encourage them, give them support, tell them they're okay, that the person who did this to them is at fault, and don't worry about it. Don't blame yourself. It's really gratifying to watch.

JERRI LYNN: I think they're like any other group of adolescents and teenagers. They're certainly cliquey — that happens — but one thing that's brought them all here together is that they're a sexual minority. There are certainly some participants who sometimes get on the other kids' nerves, but I don't think it's any different than any other group of teenagers. There could be the potential here for racial problems because 70 percent of our youth are of color — African-American,

Latino, Pacific Islander, and Native Americans — which is kind of surprising. The potential for conflict is there, but I think that teens are really good at calling one another on these things. Face it, when we look at the adults in the gay and lesbian community, we don't have a lot to be proud of when it comes to where we're at with racial or gender issues. So I think it's important that some of the program topics here specifically address racism and diversity, just to remind the kids that there are so many different colors and religions in our community.

MICHAEL: Also, not all the kids identify themselves as gay. If they come in saying they think that they're straight and that they're just interested in finding out more, or they're questioning, or they're bisexual, that's fine. They're as welcome here as anybody else. Each kid comes with a different story. Some kids have walked around the block outside several times before they get the courage to come in, or sometimes they've been outside on another night and couldn't quite make themselves get in here — it's not unlike my generation's first experience with gay bars, maybe. You just need to make them feel that they have someone here they can talk to. I think that is the most important aspect of what we do, providing them with a safe, supportive environment in which to explore their own feelings. They see that they have options. They can see that there are people here from all sorts of backgrounds, from all different walks of life, that they're not doomed to suicide at an early age or limited to a career as a hairdresser.

JERRI LYNN: There's kind of a fine line in what we do. We don't provide counseling and we don't provide therapy, because kids need parental permission for that. What we very often do is make referrals. We may have a young person who comes in who's homeless, so we make a referral to a homeless shelter. We may talk to someone who attempted suicide three weeks before, and we know they need to talk with a therapist. Probably every night we're making a referral for someone to someplace.

Some of the kids are hustling, exchanging sex for money. They're very frightened, and they're doing it because they need to survive. The ones who are doing that tend to be the homeless kids; they've been thrown out of the home because of their sexual orientation or they're not getting along with their parents, or because of their sexual orientation they got beaten up by their parents and chose to run away instead of living there. A big part of our program is HIV and AIDS education, which is important for any teenager but certainly concerns the youth who are on the street. We also have kids who drive here from Indiana because they need to get some support; we have upper-class suburban kids; we have kids who are middle-class from the city. It's just amazing.

MICHAEL: There's one kid whose mother drives him in a Mercedes from the suburbs and waits for him outside. We have somebody else who's living in a box because his father threw him out when he found out he wanted to dress like a girl. And everything in between. They can come here and be what they want to be. But then they have to go back to their high school.

JERRI LYNN: Our purpose here isn't to get them to come out of the closet. We want, if it's just for two hours a week or six hours a week, for them to feel good about themselves. That's better than not at all. Our objective isn't to have them come out at home or at school, because that could be really unsafe for them. If they have to be closeted at school instead of getting beaten up, we're going to support that. It's the same with coming out to their parents. There could be a very violent outcome, so much so that they don't have a home to live in anymore. It's too bad that they have to leave here and not be open about themselves, but that's just the reality of our society right now.

I'd say that a good portion of the youth who come here are not undecided about their sexuality — they've known all of their lives. They may not have had a label for it, but they knew they were different, and when dating time comes along and puberty hits, they're finally able to identify what that difference has been. So I would say that more youth come here who know exactly who they are than who don't. My typical response to someone who thinks that we are "luring" the kids into a lifestyle is "Why would someone choose to be a member of an oppressed group?" And just as heterosexuals know without a doubt that they have absolutely no attraction to someone of the same sex, it is the same for someone who is gay or lesbian or bisexual. You know who you're attracted to, and you can't fake it. Or you can fake it, but you can't mean it inside.

"I was out in the police academy. I think if you're really comfortable with being out, it helps other people be comfortable with it, too."

CHAPTER THREE

DOROTHY KNUDSON

Dorothy Knudson believes she was the first openly lesbian police officer on the Chicago force, and, along with some fellow officers, she has founded the Lesbian and Gay Police Associaton. Confident and articulate, Dorothy voices below what it's like to be gay and a woman in the macho world of law enforcement, where, she believes, staying in the closet is not the answer.

I always feel that being aware of being different makes me better in my job. Difference is good, especially for something like police work, because it does make you a little more sensitive — it gives you a broader point of view. You realize that there are other differences. I'm not going to say that I understand what "those people" are going through, in any situation, whoever "those people" may be, because I'm not going to dare know what it's like to be in someone else's shoes. At the same time, I understand what it's like to be in *a* different pair of shoes and be recognized as somehow different within our society, which supposedly celebrates differences. I'm still figuring that one out. It's America, where you should be what you want to be — but be like us while you're doing it. I don't let myself forget I'm different or forget I'm a lesbian. I like it. I see it as an asset, and it gives me a chance to use who I am in a good way.

When I was around seven years old, I was at the airport with my parents, probably around the holiday season. My grandparents were flying in, I think, and it was crowded. It was 1970, when everyone had long hair and loose fitting, flowered clothing. I remember two long-haired figures coming close to me, their arms wrapped around each other. And I was just assuming that it was a guy and a girl, but as they got closer, I saw it was two women. I didn't think anything about it, I didn't know what it meant, but I felt this weird churning in my stomach, and I didn't even know what *that* meant. I wasn't repelled. I had no idea, and I forgot all about it until later on in life, when I started coming out to myself, remembering that experience and knowing what that churning was.

Looking back, I always felt I was different. I wasn't an only child, but my brother, who was closest to me in age, was nine years older. When I was five, six, and seven, my siblings were already in high school, and soon they were in college. They were in a whole different world, and as far as our family structure went, things had changed so that I grew up in a different environment in terms of access to my parents and things like that. I always felt like I was kind of on the outside, struggling to be a part of my own family. I taught myself to tie my own shoes at the age of two and a half. I was the only left-handed person in my family, and they tied 'em backwards. It was this trying to be a part of things that they were doing, I think, that led me to tying my own shoes, and reading newspapers when I was little so I could talk about things at the dinner table. I was a real intense child, very serious, very emotional, and very sensitive. My feelings got hurt easy. My grade school was very cliquey, and in sixth grade I managed to fall out of the in group and felt very ostracized, very alone. I started developing better friendships in junior high.

When I began high school, I started trying to figure out those dreams I was having. They weren't really, like, graphic; they were dreams where I'd be marrying my best friend. They would be very emotional, romantic dreams. All through high school, I knew and I didn't know. I couldn't tell anybody. Or didn't want to tell anybody. What makes all this clouded is that during high school I had become a born-again Christian . . . which complicates all of these things.

I was in this youth group. I joined because my best friend was involved. She was a born-again Christian, and I started going with her on Friday nights. I think it was mostly my desire to be near *her* every waking moment that took me there. I didn't make a really good born-again Christian because I tend to question things. I don't take answers like "Because" very well or "That's beyond our realm of understanding" — no, don't tell me that. If it's within my knowledge to ask the question, then it's within my knowledge to know if there's an answer. I did enjoy the bantering back and forth about the Bible — the Bible's a great work whether you accept it as the word of God or just look at it as literature. That was always fun.

One woman, a student at a local Christian college, and I became pretty good friends. I actually told her at one point — I think I was a junior in high school — that I thought I was gay. We'd gone for a walk and I said, "Look, I really need to talk to you." I needed to talk to someone by this point 'cause — I mean, I was dating guys all through high school, but that was a game. Everybody dated somebody, and it was just fun. But what I was really feeling was strong attraction to my best friend. So this other friend and I went for a walk. Beautiful Sunday afternoon, and we ended up so we were facing each other on a set of steps. I was standing on one side; she was sitting on the other. And I told her. As far as pure and straight and narrow goes, she epitomized it, and I wasn't sure how she'd deal with it. I wasn't even sure if she knew what *lesbian* meant. But she got up and she walked across the steps and sat down next to me, which I think made a big difference in the way I was able to come out later on. That experience still touches me. She said, "Maybe we should pray about it," which is a good Christian answer to everything. You don't have an answer? We'll pray about it.

I wavered back and forth all through high school. I even thought, This is Satan doing this to you. It still scares me that I actually blamed it on Satan. I had a best friend in college where the feelings were returned, but she was straight. We were very close emotionally, more than just good friends, so it was very confusing for her and very frustrating for me — but I knew what I was. Even before I was physically involved with women, I was saying yes, this is it . . . I'm gay. And not fretting over it, just thinking, Okay. All I gotta do is find a woman.

I met my first lover in college. I was pre-med. I was going to be a doctor. My whole family had known, my entire life, that I was going to be a doctor, and I knew I was going to be a doctor — and I get to college and then suddenly I realized "I don't want to be a doctor! I don't want to do this!" So I left college, partially for financial reasons and partially because I needed a break. I'd really just come out to myself; I'd discovered a whole new world, and I was having a good time, which a lot of college students do, but for me that meant sacrificing my studies. I knew I needed some time to myself. I needed some time to grow up; I needed some time to deal with some of the other issues I was still struggling with. So I went to dispatch for a private ambulance company because I didn't want an office job. I became an EMT — emergency medical technician — because the company required their dispatchers to do that, and I started working on the ambulance from time to time. And it was fun. It was fun being out on the streets, it was fun to help people, it was fun dealing with emergency situations.

So the police department seemed like a logical next step. It had good benefits, it's exciting, it's different, I get to deal with people, and I get to help people. I thought I could bring something in there, maybe an amount of patience or respect that would help me understand more what crime victims, especially women, have to deal with. What do you mean, why was she walking down the street at three in the morning? She lives on this planet! Men walk down the street at three in the morning. It's a very "take back the night" thing for me.

I was out in the police academy. I think I'm so used to being out, I'm comfortable with it. Being out for me is very important. I think if you're really comfortable with being out, it helps other people be comfortable with it, too. When I decided to try police work, I knew I'd be out, and I thought, Well, how am I going to be able to be out in the police department? because I couldn't imagine it being a very open place. But then I couldn't imagine myself not being out, so I figured the two would just work out fine. And they have.

Sometimes I'll talk about it just so someone knows. I can be talking to someone for the first time, and I'll mention my girlfriend, Rhonda, or something and just work it into normal conversation the way anybody would. Sometimes you see that little puzzled look on people's faces for a second, but then they just shrug it off. My shift partners are all fine with it. I've had a couple of people who'd ask questions like "Oh, you are? Well, how did you know?" or "When did it happen?" (I like that one) or "Did something happen to you to make you this way?" They're legitimate questions. There are so many myths, and unless you open communication, you're not going to be able to dispel the

myths. Just being me and being out helps break down some of the myths.

I chose the twenty-third district, where a lot of gay people live, as my training district for the academy because I thought being out and being a recruit are tough. It's always hard being a new kid anywhere. And they call you the new kid even if you're forty. So I came here, and I thought, Well, the cops in this neighborhood deal with gays and lesbians all the time. They'll be more accepting. They were very nice to me, although they talked about me a lot behind my back. For some reason that district has a big rumor mill. And they would say things that weren't necessarily true, which is funny, because I say enough things that I would have thought they didn't have to make stuff up. I gave everybody plenty of material to work with! Where I am now, in the eleventh district, they don't really talk about me behind my back, at least not on my watch.

Once I was talking with another police officer, and he was using the word *faggot*. I got pissed at him because I was standing right there and I was just assuming he knew by now because I've told a *lot* of people. I told him, "Just cut the crap," and walked away. He says, "Well, what do you care?" I gave him a dirty look and walked out, and my partner said, "She's a lesbian." "*I* didn't know that," and then he apologized to me. Of course he still didn't understand why I took offense at *faggot*; he hadn't used the word *dyke*. No, no, no. Derogatory words and comments about gay men are still one of the last bastions of acceptable insults within our society, not just in the police force. It's like being around a lot of little boys on the playground. "You're a sissy." "You're a faggot."

There are gay men on the force. I finally met one who would admit to me that he was gay. There's no reason to believe the percentage of gay people in the police department is any different from general society. Ten percent sounds like a reasonable number. I think police are better at hiding it. Being in a macho profession is a way of hiding it. I think some of those who are most derogatory are also the most conflicted, and they certainly don't want anyone else to suspect. There are other lesbians in the district who unfortunately I still don't know. They avoid me like the plague. A lot of the police lesbians who seem to avoid me are the older women who have paid their dues. They were some of the first women on the job. They put up with a lot of hassling. Men didn't want to work with them — there were a lot of comments about "that time of the month again," really rude comments. They had to go through all that, and they forged a path, and they're on the beaten path now. I'm kind of wandering off the path.

Arresting women is sort of like a *Thelma and Louise* syndrome for me. I think, Well, of course she did it. She *should* do it. All of us should be out here doing this shit. I once arrested a woman who went off on this guy and started hitting him in front of us. Don't hit someone in front of the police, because you don't leave us a lot of choice. You're committing a crime in front of us. She was a huge woman, and this was a hard fight. The hardest thing about it was that her kids were there, her little ones. That's the toughest thing, hearing "Mommy, Mommy, don't hurt my mommy." And you want to say, "Oh, I don't want to hurt your mommy, honey, I won't hurt her." Meanwhile, Mommy is swinging me across her living room. "I'm not going to hurt her. If she'll just put me down, I won't hurt her." Finally after she calms down and we have to go to the station, she starts telling us about all this shit this guy has been doing to her. She had no visible marks on her, and it gets hard to believe anybody, but I still tend to believe women first.

Hate crimes, where penalties for assault are increased if it can be proven that the attack was motivated by prejudice, are a rallying concern in the gay and lesbian community today. But I'm afraid I don't exactly share the "politically correct" point of view. If somebody breaks my window because I'm a lesbian, and somebody breaks my neighbor's for no particular reason, we both still have to replace the window. I at least have the satisfaction of knowing *why* my window was broken, where my neighbor might spend the rest of her life wondering why this happened to her. I think that's a lot scarier. I do think it's vitally important to keep accurate statistics on hate crimes. The only way to prevent crime is to understand it. But sufficient penalties are already on the books — they're just not used enough by the courts, which, in my opinion, are often too lenient in general when it comes to sentencing offenders.

My lover worries about me, especially if I'm late and I don't call. If I'm due off in a half hour but make an arrest that's going to take an hour's worth of paperwork, I gotta call her — "I'm going to be a little late" — because otherwise she imagines the worst. I think that's another reason why I've been so out. If something does happen to me, I don't want any doubts about who she is or who's to be notified. On every one of my emergency notification cards, I've listed her as my lover. I don't want any doubts about who this person is or what she means to me, the importance she has in my life. I don't want them to think they're just calling my roommate, who could be, if I move every year, someone different. This is the person I'm spending my life with. Part of the reason I'm so out is for her.

CHAPTER FOUR

TERRENCE SMITH

Terrence — aka drag artist Joan Jett Blakk — is an articulate and provocative spokesman for what he calls "queer" visibility. It's the kind of talk that makes many straight people — not to mention a whole lot of gay people — nervous. In most local gay papers, for example, a letter or two will appear before the annual gay pride parade politely asking that this year, please, would the drag queens and leathermen and dykes-on-bikes please stay home? We have to start worrying about our image. As Terrence modestly asserts, "I exist to explode that."

I was a big sissy when I was a kid. I wouldn't do anything that would even remotely get me dirty. I was not into scrapes, bruises, cuts, any of that. I wanted my clothes to be perfect, as perfect when I came home as they'd been when I left the house. And I was not interested in any of the stuff that boys did. You know, playing chicken on bikes — I didn't do any of that. I'm like, "This is a brand-new bike. Get away from it. You are not going to bash up my brand-new bike." I was the weird kid down the street. I remember when I was twelve or something, and my parents went out and left me in the house alone. *You* know where I went? Right to my mother's jewelry box. Did I know why? No. I just knew that I went right to her jewelry box and I was trying on the earrings. I don't know why, because there was nothing beforehand that made me want to do that. I just knew that she always wore this fun jewelry and I wanted to get in there and see what it looked like on me. So I did. It was fun, you know? I knew it was going to be fun, and part of the fun was that you could easily get caught. There you were in your *mother's room* in her *jewelry box* and you were the *boy.* That was more trouble than you could ever imagine. But still, it pulled me. I went to see the Supremes when I was nine years old, and I was taken aback by

their beauty, and I didn't know why. I just knew that I loved it. I could lip-synch already to every Supremes record I knew. I can remember watching *What Ever Happened to Baby Jane?* when I was ten years old and really getting off on Bette Davis saying, "But y'*are*, Blanche. Y'*are*." Gay kids just pick right up on it, and turn around and go, "But y'*are*." You know, straight boys can't do that. You can definitely tell a straight boy by how he holds a cigarette. Straight boys hold cigarettes differently from gay boys; it's just a little bit more of a flourish we have, and that's good. Difference is good.

Until the fourth grade, I was the only black kid in my class. I was going to Catholic school in the mid-'60s, when the one thing they wanted most in the world was a black kid in their class. I kind of picked up on that early — that's why I'm such a media whore now, because I know when to raise my hand. There was nothing more exciting than having them go, "Who wants to wash the board?" "I do!" "Let's get Terrence," right? So I became this little example they could hold up and say, "See, we got a black kid! Right there! Right there!" And I'm like, "Okay, I'll work this. This is fun." I used to want to be a priest. Like almost every other good Catholic boy, I was an altar boy, and I thought, This guy's got a really cool job. He sits over there in the rectory all day, he drives a Lincoln, the nuns wait on him hand and foot, and all he does is come over and wave at us every so often, and we're like, "Wow, it's Father."

When it came time for high school, my parents decided, Well, we'll send him to a black school. I was under the impression this would be easy, right? "Oh, black kids. Okay, no problem." I started in September, and that January I transferred because I couldn't stand it anymore. At least once a week I would have some incident with one of those kids. They beat my ass, they would pull my stuff out of my locker, because I wasn't black like they were black. I didn't talk like them; I didn't have the same interests as they did. I remember that Halloween we were supposed to bring records to play at school. They brought Sly and the Family Stone, and all this stuff, which is great music, but I brought Alice Cooper. And they broke my records. I was always being hassled by the guys at school before school would start, so I would try to find a place to hide before the bell rang. And for some bizarre reason the key to the front door of our house worked in the lock to the church. So I could go and sit in church and read until the bell. I felt that there was some force watching that was kind of there to protect me. I could hide from everybody.

I used to spend a lot of time in the library, because I wasn't a very sports-oriented kid — I had no time for that sort of stuff. (Take baseball. You hit the ball, then you run over there, over there, over there, back here. I'm like, "I'm already here." My dad bought me a basketball net and put it up on the garage, and he says, "This ball goes in there." "Why is it way up there? Why isn't it down here?" I went and got a ladder.) I became addicted to magazines. I would read *Vogue*, and *Bazaar, Interview,* all these magazines. So one day I'm looking through a *Vogue* magazine, and I see a picture of David Bowie. Well, for some strange reason at sixteen years old I fall madly in love with this guy, and I don't know why. I hadn't thought about guys, I hadn't thought about girls, I didn't believe sex was possible. We had sex education in the eighth grade, and I didn't believe it. I was like, "You gotta be kidding. You mean — no. You mean I have to like get on top — no, no, no, this can't be it. They're lying to me. I'm not doing that." But I absolutely fell totally in love with this man who was the most beautiful creature I had ever seen, and I had heard that he was "gay." Since I was in the library already, I thought, well, let me look this up, *gay.* Hmm, okay. *Homosexual.* Hmm. Okay. I looked it up and I found what it meant, and I figured well, I must be one, too. I'm sitting in the library thinking, Well, he's gay and I'm gay, but I don't see any other gay people around. I see David Bowie and I see myself.

I didn't know what gay people looked like or where they were or what they did or anything, so I spent the next year or so kind of trying to figure out who I was. I started going to David Bowie concerts, and meeting other people. By the time I was in the tenth grade, I was wearing silver platform boots and had no eyebrows, and I was this hardcore glitter kid. My parents were, I'm sure, starting to wonder about those pictures of David Bowie all over my room. They were starting to wonder, Wait a minute, what's going on here? This isn't what we wanted from our firstborn son. But, you know, I was recently talking to my mother, and she said she had no idea I was gay before I told them. I said, "Ma, you had no idea? I had pictures of David Bowie up all over my room, you had no idea? All I could talk about when I was five years old was Jackie Kennedy, and you had no idea? Come on!" Of course parents, they don't have that learning either. They just figure, "That's my weird child." But we've come full circle now. My parents are actually thinking about joining P-FLAG [Parents, Families and Friends of Lesbians and Gays], and I'm very happy about that.

I know a lot of people who are younger than me who didn't discover themselves so easily. It was a very painful thing for them. But for me, I always say that I didn't come out of the closet — I, like, kicked the door down. And then turned around and painted it, redecorated it, and left.

I hatched Joan Jett Blakk for an ACT-UP demonstration in 1990, when we did street theater in front of Cook County Hospital to protest their policies with AIDS patients. I had done drag many years before in Detroit, but I wanted to do something different. Drag itself is different from female impersonation, with its illusion of "Oh my God, I *know* that's a boy, but he looks so much like a woman." Drag is like, "That's a man! In a dress!" And I always had rock-and-roll leanings in the performances I did. Back in Detroit I used to do Kiki Dee and Grace Jones and Janis Joplin, but I wanted a new name. So I was sitting around with a friend and we were talking about different names, and somehow we came up with Betty White Black, which just didn't sound right. And then I don't remember which one of us it was, but we found it: "Joan Jet Black!" So it stuck. It's spelled different, but it stuck.

I always call myself the Goddess of Love. No bitchiness, even backstage, none of that. Because drag queens can be really mean to each other. And I don't like being mean at all; I think it's unnecessary. So I would always be really sweet and everything. And that's the kind of persona I have. Even though Joan *is* kind of menacing, Joan is menacing because she's an in-your-face drag queen. Not because she's going to say something to you that's going to cut you down, it's not about that. Joan is menacing because she's there in a fishnet body stocking.

And that's pretty scary in itself. When I'm in drag I can say things that I probably wouldn't otherwise say to total strangers. It gives me this extra armor to be able to say anything I want to to anyone. I can talk to Joan, but nobody else can. Somebody will ask me, "You think Joan wants to do that?" "Let me talk to her. We'll see." I'm her liaison. Sometimes I'll be walking down the street with somebody and there'll be a great dress in the window and I'm saying, "I should talk to Joan — she would love that dress." Obviously I'm saying "*I* want that dress!"

Joan ran for president, on the Queer Nation ticket, in 1988. No one else had thought of a drag queen running for president before. Don't ask me — the Goddess was with me — but somehow we came up with this, and we decided to really go with it. It took drag to a different place, which is exactly what I wanted to do. I wanted to take drag out of the idea of lip-synching in front of a microphone or a whore working the streets, which is something else that some drag queens do, you know. I wanted to take it away from there and put it someplace else. To put it in the political arena was perfect, because elections are kind of beauty contests anyway, kind of a bizarre beauty contest, and I figured, well, let's add some *real* beauty to the contest.

The places that I ended up as a presidential candidate are not the kind of places I would have ended up as just a drag performer. I met Geraldine Ferraro, Paul Tsongas. I went to the Democratic convention. It was really scary. It was one of the scariest things I've ever done. I don't usually get nervous when I'm in drag, but believe me, being inside Madison Square Garden for the convention was frightening. Because you're right there in the belly of the beast. There were all these power brokers there, and it made my flesh crawl to be around all these politicians. They're kind of yucky people, as a rule. I went with a gay cable network and they thought it would be a great thing to have the queer presidential candidate, Queer Nation's presidential candidate, on the floor of the Democratic convention. Infiltrating. So I went into the bathroom, the men's bathroom in Madison Square Garden, and put my makeup on in a stall. It's a lot of makeup to put on, eyelashes and everything. So I'm putting it on, I'm finishing up, and I'm wearing a red, white, and blue miniskirt, and my favorite black seven-inch stiletto heels from Frederick's of Hollywood, which make me a rather tall person. I'm five-six, and it's nice to be over six feet tall for once. I'm sitting in the stall, and I hear a guard outside the stall say, "Hey! Hey! This is the men's bathroom!" and so I had to say "It *is* a man in here," and came out. I wish you could have seen the look on this guard's face — it was priceless. I looked right at him, said "Thank you," and walked right on out onto the main floor. I've got a press pass, so they can't do anything. Just as we get inside the door, they announce Mario Cuomo. The lights go out, the audience screams, and it looked like they were cheering for *me*. And of course I milk that. Suddenly I was standing in front of a whole half-circle of cameras and microphones and everything. I got to talk about being Queer Nation's presidential candidate, and I took pictures with a lot of delegates. I'm sure most of the people had no idea who I was, so they probably went back home and said, "Yeah, well, I don't know, we took a picture with this black guy in a dress — I don't know who it was."

But I got a chance to get our message across about visibility. Because that's why we did it. We did it for queer visibility. For no other reason. People say, well, you know, "gays and lesbians," well, gays and lesbians are fine, but we want *queer* visibility. We want the people who *are* different. We're trying to let everyone know that we're here, too. Not just the gay people who say, "We're just like you. We want to have a house and kids just like you." Well, a lot of people aren't like that, and that's who I kind of represent. The fact that we are different is what makes us so special, and it makes being gay very special. It's not just this accident of nature — it's this wonderful thing that's happened. I don't know why it happened, and I don't care why it happened. It's not as linear as being heterosexual. You can do anything you want. Not that being tied down to raising kids is bad, but in order for a society to really grow, you have to have people who aren't tied down. It's not an accident that lots of gay men and gay women are artists and writers and painters and musicians, because they're able to channel their whole lives into this beauty as opposed to channeling their whole lives into raising kids.

If I want to wear lipstick, why not? I look great in lipstick. People have such a hard time with that concept. They think men should dress like men and women should dress like women. I exist to explode that.

"That's a man! In a dress!"

Because who decided that? And why should we just blindly go along with it? It just doesn't make any sense to me. I did a radio interview in Dublin, Ireland, and believe me, they were hysterical. They couldn't believe that a black drag queen was running for president in the United States. They were freaking out. One of the guys said to me, "Well, why are you doing this in a dress?" And I said, "Because I can." He said, "Well, I'd love to run for president, and I don't have a dress." And I said, "Go get one!" It's that simple.

CHAPTER FIVE

YVONNE ZIPTER

One aspect of community is that you do things together. This is both cause and effect — you do things together because you want to be with other gay people, and by being together, whether for a softball game, gay chorus, or volunteer work, you reinforce and even deepen community, giving you and the other participants something else in common besides being gay. Many cities have gay choruses; even more, reckons Yvonne Zipter, have lesbian softball teams. Why softball? I asked Yvonne to talk about softball and other cultural phenomena in the lesbian community, which overlaps the gay men's community but is in many ways distinct. Yvonne is an editor and writer in Chicago. She is the author of The Patience of Metal, *a book of poetry, and her book* Diamonds Are a Dyke's Best Friend *is a cross-country survey of the lesbian softball phenomenon.*

Besides softball, there are very few other things that you can say about the lesbian community that are so universal. Softball for some reason seems to be *the* sport. I don't know if there's a way to actually prove this, but I think that just after the turn of the century, there were all these reform movements going on, with social workers trying to get better working conditions for people in the factories and whatnot. Part of their program was to institute recreation programs for people working in factories, and part of this was softball. Among the women working in those days, chances are a lot of them were lesbians, because in the '20s and '30s, and maybe into the early '40s, married women did not work outside of the home unless there were dire circumstances. I think word sort of spread that softball was a way you could meet other lesbians, because in those days there weren't many other places to meet lesbians. And later, in the '40s and '50s, there weren't many bars, and when there were, it was always a risk because you never knew when

"Lesbians were always in the background, so it's been neat for people to realize that we exist, too."

there was going to be a raid. So softball was sort of a safe place to meet other women. It wasn't necessarily that all women on the team were lesbians, but you were likely to find at least a few lesbians on any given women's softball team.

Also, softball's a sport based on baseball, the national pastime, so most everybody has some conception of how you play the game. Everybody kind of grows up seeing softball and baseball played all around them on playgrounds, on TV. I think that all of that goes into why lesbians play softball. In big urban areas, softball's not the only place you can go to meet other lesbians. There are a billion other places. But in the rural areas, from the few people that I've talked to, it still works the way it did in the '40s and '50s. They don't have bars and coffeehouses and bookstores and all those places to congregate. There's just softball. In South Dakota and North Dakota and places like that, some of those women will travel fifty miles or more just to play softball, and they find each other on the teams.

When I was a kid, I wasn't doing a lot of the traditional male sports or anything; I was just real active, doing a lot of tree climbing and bike riding. I had a pogo stick and all that kind of stuff, but once I hit junior high, I started getting a lot of pressure, subtle and not so subtle, to start acting like a lady. In junior high I had this big bike that had been my mom's, a big old Schwinn with balloon tires; now those bikes are kind of cool, but then, *nobody* wanted to be seen on a bike like that. And all I wanted was a new bike with coaster brakes and skinny tires; I didn't want anything fancy. I had to argue with my parents for a long time because they said, "You won't be riding that much longer."

I had feelings toward girls pretty early. I didn't know much about being gay or lesbian; I just knew it wasn't a good thing. I remember developing crushes on a wide array of women and girls as early as junior high and high school, but I blocked it all out and rationalized it. I said to myself, Well, when I think about these girls or these women, I'm thinking about holding their hand or hugging them or something, and that's not sexual, and therefore I'm not a homosexual. I had this whole elaborate rationale worked out for myself. I convinced myself that I sort of had crushes on some boys at school and tried to whip up some interest in them, but I would have been much better off just being friends with them. It was pretty clear that my strongest emotional ties were with women. I successfully fought that until toward the end of college sometime, where I was in a class with this woman who kept talking about being a lesbian all the time, and I didn't particularly like her style; she referred to her girlfriend as her "old lady," and it scared me a little. Then I met somebody who I fell head over heels in love with. At that point I just sort of felt like, Well, if I'm a lesbian, so what?

I decided to play softball after college when I was living out in the suburbs and did not know a single other lesbian. So I said to myself, If they're going to be anywhere out here, they're going to be playing softball. And so I joined a team affiliated with the place where I was working, Bell Labs. There were around ten women's teams, because it's a big place. Still, I never *did* meet any other lesbians while I was playing out there — so much for my theories!

When I moved into the city, I finally found a lesbian team, in fact a whole league. The first team I was on was really competitive, and sometimes I felt so intimidated by how good they were that I don't think I played my best. Not all the teams are that competitive. I met a woman who's in the physical education department at the University of Massachusetts, and she plays in a league that describes itself as feminist. They have a lot of rules. Everybody gets to play; winning is not the object. If somebody is disabled or has trouble with her knees and can't run, she can have somebody run for her after she bats. I forget what the other rules are, but it's very different. I believe they keep score, but sometimes when one team is clearly better than the other, they just mix up their players after a couple innings. They say, Well, it's clear that we're going to tromple all over you," and they just mix up the teams so it would be a more evenly matched game. It's a very different attitude.

I like lesbian softball because I can be totally at ease. I think if I were playing on a team with straight women or with men, I'd be much more self-conscious. In my experience, lesbian teams — even the more competitive ones — tend to be fairly supportive. And you can be very out and open about who you are, so that's not an issue. Being gay is not an element of the game, but in terms of socializing before and after games

and practices and whatnot, it's just a nice feeling. It's validating, in some ways, to be surrounded by lesbians. It's an experience I never grow tired of. Depending on my state of mind, I can get really sappy about it. There's just something that feels good about knowing there are that many other strong, independent, caring women around you.

By the time I found my first lesbian softball team, I'd also found a women's coffeehouse and a women's bookstore. I got used to being surrounded by lesbians a lot. These days, it feels like we're everywhere. We certainly have been in the news a lot. It's pretty wild. News shows like *20/20* — every time you turn around there's another lesbian thing on there. It's exciting and weird all at the same time, just to finally be *noticed*. People had been paying a lot more attention to gay men over the years, not necessarily positive attention, but recognizing that they exist. Lesbians were always in the background, so it's been neat for people to realize that we exist, too. But it sort of makes you feel like a circus freak, you know? And it's pretty glamorized, this whole lesbian chic thing. Melissa Etheridge and k.d. lang coming out and getting a lot of attention has really glamorized being a lesbian. I never thought I'd be glamorous. But that's sort of nice, too, because one of the stereotypes always was that we were these big hulking bulldaggers dressed in flannel shirts with key rings hanging off our belt loops, so it's nice for people to have a different image. Not that it's not any more accurate. There's been a lot of emphasis on lesbians having babies and raising families and being regular, too, and that kind of attention is probably even better.

There's also been more openness within the lesbian community itself. I think the community is less rigid from a political standpoint than it used to be. In the beginning it was very important for lesbians to be able to define themselves in a positive way that was distinct from the rest of the culture, because so much of our society defines lesbians in a negative way. I think lesbians developed a political structure that gave us a certain amount of strength and focus and purpose, but that could sometimes be authoritarian — you know, this is *the* way to be a lesbian, the whole politically correct thing. The political stance has been softening over the years in terms of dress, for example, but as far as racism and sexism go, there's still a pretty strong contingent that believes it's very important to stay vigilant.

Younger lesbians seem to be much more up-front about their sexuality. I think they have a much easier time talking about sex than most older lesbians did. I was raised in a pretty puritanical household, so I'm a little uncomfortable with it myself, but it's better for people to be able to talk about that kind of stuff openly than not. Everything is so eroticized now, and things have gotten wilder in lesbian bars. Even though the bar crowd was never overwhelmingly feminist, I think there used to be a lot of pressure not to "objectify" women. You weren't supposed to like pretty women; that was considered being a "looksist." There was a strong feminist tenet against doing that, but people are loosening up — that's part of this whole relaxing of the political structure in the lesbian community.

People still argue about the whole lesbian separatist thing, where you aim to keep men out of your life as much as possible. I just don't think that separatism is quite the issue that it used to be. Gay men and lesbians are closer then they were, but there's lots of room for improvement. There aren't a lot of good venues for overlap between the men and women, unless it's through AIDS work. I just don't see enough opportunities for the two parts of the community to come together. But it's definitely better than it used to be.

It's a difficult issue. I think that lesbians, for whatever reason, do have a different consciousness from most gay men and are more aware, in some ways, of the inequities in the American legal and political system in a way that gay men, at least the ones who are white and make good money, are not. They don't have the same experience of being discriminated against that a lot of lesbians do. Lesbians tend to be more committed to ensuring that everyone gets treated equally along the way. Sometimes you can get over-concerned with that stuff and not get something accomplished as efficiently as you might have. But you have to be real careful when you assume what another person wants. Gay and lesbian opinion is hardly monolithic. Take domestic partnership legislation. Some gays and lesbians think that the whole institution of marriage needs to be torn apart and revamped and that marriage is not something that we should be emulating. Another group feels, okay, but in the meantime, all these married people are getting these rights and we don't. I certainly hope we're not emulating all aspects of heterosexual marriages, but getting together in a committed, monogamous relationship is something that feels natural to a lot of people.

I'm hooked up on a computer network of people discussing gay and lesbian issues, and there was a whole heated debate going about abortion rights that divided on gender lines: the women could *not* understand how gay men could not understand why being pro-choice was a lesbian issue, and gay men could not understand how lesbians could think it *was* a lesbian issue. I don't think anybody got convinced of anything. There was another debate about breast cancer. As with abortion rights, I believe that it is a lesbian issue, even more so in some ways. Statistically, lesbians are one of the populations that are more likely to get breast cancer because they tend not to breast-feed at an early age, and they also tend to have trouble finding gynecologists that they can feel comfortable with, so they don't get breast exams as regularly as they should. More research needs to be done, but I think there is a link. It's not as if one could say breast cancer strikes only lesbians, but on the other hand, AIDS doesn't affect only gay men — there are larger populations involved. I don't know that it's an exactly parallel analogy, but I think there are similarities. A lot of these men were saying, "Well, I don't believe it's a lesbian issue, but I am supportive. I do believe we should do stuff about breast cancer." So I said, "Okay, I'm going to hold you to that when the next lesbian cancer project benefit comes up." I want to see your money where your mouth is, guys!

CHAPTER SIX

ED KASSING

"Don't ask, don't tell," was a phrase heard and argued on the news and on the talk shows and in the newspaper while the Senate was conducting hearings in 1993 on President Clinton's proposal to lift the ban on gays and lesbians serving in the military. Several stories were prominent: Margarethe Cammermeyer, a decorated Navy nurse, was forced out for her admission of her lesbianism; Allen Schindler was serving in Japan when he was beaten to death by a shipmate who allegedly taunted him about his homosexuality while he killed him. As Ed Kassing points out below, the debate is not really about letting gays and lesbians into the military. "We're already there," he says; the issue is actually whether an enlistee can be honest about who he or she is. The "don't ask, don't tell" policy is meant to be a compromise between those who believe gays should be able to serve openly and those who believe homosexuality is incompatible with military service. Although gays and lesbians are thankful that the policy has meant recruiters no longer ask potential soldiers about their sexual orientation, it remains unclear what could happen if a soldier's homosexuality becomes known.

During high school, I intended on going to college, but then my family told me they were not going to help me pay for it. They said that I would appreciate it more if I paid for it myself. I decided to go into the military because of the educational benefits they offered, around twelve thousand dollars, and I also wanted to travel. I wanted to go to Europe. So I signed up.

I was eighteen when I went in, but at that point I hadn't really thought about my sexuality. There were a couple of questions on the entrance application — I forget how it was worded — along the lines of "Do you now or have you ever had homosexual tendencies?" And

"I would have been thrown out of the army very fast."

then there was another that came right out and said, "Are you a homosexual?" I just checked off "No" to these questions. I hadn't really thought about it. In high school, there was a girl that I had chased after for four years and thought I was really in love with, but it turned out to be really more of a friendship, a brother-sister relationship. I guess about two weeks after I went into the military, I was home on vacation for Christmas and was out shopping with a friend and she said, "You know, so-and-so's gay," and I was like, "Whoa, wait a minute." This guy happened to be one of my best friends from high school, and I had no idea. That's what really made me stop and think about my own sexuality. And then I was terrified, and I went to my father and I told him. I was terrified, you know, because I had just signed this statement for the military that said if you're found out, you can go to jail for being homosexual in the military *and* for lying on this statement. I had just joined up, and I was going to be in for *six years*. And my dad told me, "Well, you just keep it under wraps, and go on like nothing's wrong. Do your time and then get out and you won't have to worry about it." My father was very good about it. He told me that I was his son, and regardless of what I chose, he would always love me.

When you're going through basic training, you think it's the hardest thing you've ever done. There are drill sergeants constantly on your back: push-ups, sit-ups, two-mile runs, carrying a forty-pound rucksack, walking fifteen miles to go to play warrior or something like that. It's awful. But then when it's done, you say, "It was a cakewalk." They're testing you to see how much stress you can take. If you just remember that it's all a big mind game, you can make it through it with no problem. The training also helped me. I was extremely overweight when I went into the military, and I lost about eighty pounds. I did physical training three times a day, six days a week for about the first month and a half that I was in the army, and every time we went to chow, I had to show the drill sergeant what I was eating to get everything approved. It was hard at the time, but now I thank them. It really got me in shape, and I never felt better.

But I had nightmares when I was in basic training, because at that point I used to talk in my sleep and I was afraid that I was going to say *something*. Somebody's always awake watching the barracks to make sure nothing's going on. I was petrified that I was going to sit up in bed and just start blabbing on about something or other and the fire guard would hear and go and tell the drill sergeant and then I would end up going to jail. It was terrifying. I really hadn't had any gay experiences yet, but I was thinking about it all the time, you know, Is this what I want?

At that point I hadn't even thought much about the military attitude toward homosexuals because I hadn't really even been able to deal with my own sexuality yet. I couldn't say, "Okay, I'm gay. I don't understand why the military doesn't like it." At that point I was still learning about myself, and I didn't deal with how the military felt about it until much later. It was at least a year before I really became comfortable with who I was. I went to Denver for training in photography. I spent six months there learning the basics of photography, everything from camera maintenance, machine maintenance, shooting black-and-white, color, processing by hand, processing by machine, all different aspects of photography. It was like being in college. That's when I went out and started trying to get a social life. I had been thinking about being gay all the time, you know: Is this what I want? Finally I experimented with it, and that's when I really came to the decision, "This is what I want." And then I also had the realization that I had to keep it hidden, because if I was caught, I could be thrown out of the military and I would lose everything that I went into the military for. I could have been thrown in jail.

When I went to my post in Germany, I kept everything kind of hidden and even started dating a girl as a front. She didn't know anything, but I knew, and nothing really happened between us. But everybody knew that I was seeing a girl, so that kept them from suspecting me. It was wrong. I look back on it, and I shouldn't have done it, but at that point I didn't want to risk my career. I felt bad because I was deceiving her; she wanted to get married and come back to the States, and I had no intention of that happening.

When I was in Germany, I told the truth about myself only to a few very close friends that I knew I could trust. It took several months of getting to know these people and building a trust with them before I

could tell them. And after that, it was just fine. It didn't change anything; they treated me just like everybody else. It didn't matter. But you had to be careful. I had a security clearance, and I would have been thrown out of the army very fast because of my job and what was entailed in my job. I did classified briefings for headquarters, and it was something you had to be very cautious of. What they say about gays being a security risk, I don't believe that in the least. I would never do anything to sabotage the military or the government. I took an oath when I went into the military. Regardless of what feelings I had, and the fact that I lied on my entrance papers and everything, I still took the military very seriously, and when I swore to obey and defend my country against all enemies foreign and domestic, I meant it. And if somebody were to try to blackmail me because they knew I was gay and they were going to go and tell the command, I would go and tell the command first. I would be kicked out, but the enemy wouldn't get any secrets.

I had good experiences with the military in general. They've given me educational benefits, and I spent two years in Germany and saw Europe. It was a learning experience. They taught me discipline; they taught me to be independent. I don't have to depend on anybody for anything. I look at the military as being a good influence on my life. It's helped me in my job, where I'm at right now, managing a camera store. I got promoted about three months ago, and it's because of the way I run things. And it all goes back to the military. I don't like to use the word *militaristic,* but everything is done in a certain way, to be the most efficient.

I think the military as an institution is a good thing. Actually, I think it should be almost like it is in Germany, where teenage boys go into the military for at least eighteen months. It teaches discipline; we wouldn't have a lot of the problems that we have in society right now with drugs and gangs and people who have no self-discipline. But it should be your choice. If you want to go into the military, that's great. But I think it should be an option for everybody, gay or straight.

Toward the end of my time in Germany, I actually started meeting other gay people in the military. I knew there were gays in the military, but I thought there were very few of them. I thought it would depend on their job — I mean, you heard rumors that the people who worked in the medical field, that most of them were gay, and the women who were MPs were gay, but it wasn't always true. You had your suspicions. When I found out that there were a lot more gay people in the military than I had thought there were, I became a little more confident about myself, because I knew that there were other people like me out there. I would say that at least 5 percent of people in the military are gay. Funny thing, once I got back to the States and was stationed in Louisiana, my roommate was gay. A post of 16,000 people, and I get put in a room with another gay man.

I don't think the "don't ask, don't tell" policy is anything new. It's just legitimizing what's already there. One thing that's nice is that they don't ask on the entrance forms anymore whether you're gay. But if they find out once you're in, you can still be kicked out. Clinton's so-called compromise didn't do anything. He totally backed down on what he said he was going to do. And I don't think the issue is going to be dropped until something more is done. I belong to GLBVA, which is the Gay, Lesbian, and Bisexual Veterans of America, and we're going to fight this until he drops the ban or does something that's a little more of a compromise than what he did, because what he did is not a compromise at all.

Basically what GLBVA is trying to do right now is to let the public know that there are gay vets. Our numbers have really increased. If people knew how many gay people are actually in the military, their minds probably would be changed. It's not like the military says — you know, less than 1 percent.

It's really pathetic, because if they were to lose all of the gay members in the military, they're going to lose some of their top, brightest individuals. A lot of good soldiers are going to be put out of service. You know, people running radar systems, and very important jobs in the military — they're going to lose all these people. And it's senseless! They're doing their job; they've been doing their job for years. And it's not affected the military. People think the issue is about letting gays into the military, but we're already there. We've been there for *years*.

I had a crush on one of my commanders. He was happily married with kids and everything. I learned to deal with it. I kept my emotions to myself. Sure, I had feelings toward other soldiers, but I *never* would have made any kind of move on them. Because that would mean throwing your career right out the window. Once I got back from Germany and I was in Louisiana, I almost got an "I don't care" attitude. I had gone past my three years in service, and after three years, if they kick you out, you still retain your benefits. That's when I had my ears pierced (couldn't wear earrings with the uniform, though!), and I had pinups of men hanging on the wall in my room. The battalion commander would walk through the barracks on inspection and see the posters up on the wall and wouldn't say anything. I guess because I was a photographer they would just chalk it up to "Oh, it's photography — it's artistic." Part of why they let me get away with a lot of the things I did was because of the position I was in, being the post photographer. In Louisiana I was the only military photographer on the post, and eventually everybody went before a promotion board and had to come to me to get their pictures taken. Their careers were in my hands! So most of the time they were very nice to me.

If I was talking to a gay seventeen-year-old now about going into the service, I would tell him or her to really think about it. Because it's a big gamble. I don't know, there are different types of gay people. If you're very outgoing and forward about who and what you are, you would be put out immediately. But if you're the type who's very quiet, keeps to yourself, and that the average person would not suspect, you could probably go through the military and nobody would ever know.

The only thing ending the ban would do is allow gays to stop worrying about being thrown out. That would relieve a lot of stress off of the homosexuals in the military. When you're gay and in the military, you have the stress of being found out and being kicked out. You also have the stress of your actual job. There's so much piled on top of you, and if they would drop the ban, and just let you be openly gay, you could perform your job better because you wouldn't have to worry about who you are. Nothing else would change. The military would continue with its mission. That's the primary thing. The mission comes first. The mission, then the unit, then the individual. That's the way you're trained. Nothing would change.

CHAPTER SEVEN

JUDITH JOHNS

In her current position as AIDS commissioner for the city of Chicago, Judith Johns continues a health career that has paralleled the spread of the AIDS epidemic and encompassed the frequently volatile social, sexual, political, and educational issues surrounding it. In her work as a hospice director, later as the director of the Howard Brown Memorial Clinic (a health center for gay men and focus for AIDS research), and in her present job, Judith has had to speak to diverse problems and audiences, preventing the spread of AIDS where it can be prevented and helping those already infected to lead as healthy and fulfilling lives as possible. "The risk of teenagers getting AIDS is probably the worst dilemma we deal with," says Judith, and here she talks about the difficulties surrounding teen sexuality and safe-sex education.

In 1980 I was hired to start a hospice program at Northwestern Memorial Hospital. The program began in 1981, and I saw my first patient with GRID — Gay-Related Immunodeficiency Disease, as it was called at the time — in 1982. I became tremendously fascinated with the disease for several reasons. Probably the most compelling was that many of these men who were facing this disease were dying very very quickly. As a matter of fact, most of the clients I saw in the beginning never made it beyond their first hospitalization. They would enter the hospital with pneumocystis, and their families would be called in, and they had a very short time to live. So within an incredibly small space of time, they were put in the position of dealing with a fatal disease as well as dealing with their families — who in almost all cases were not aware that the individual was gay. In addition to all the things families face when someone is dying, here was an added component: reconciling the guilt. And not necessarily the guilt of the person who had GRID but the guilt of the family: what could I have done to save my son? I did

"We can't be afraid to give kids information about sex."

a lot of work with the families, and that was what was most compelling to me.

In hospice work, I experienced about 350 deaths a year. Every person I saw in the beginning years with GRID died. Our job was to be there, and part of that job is to sit death vigils with the family, if the family was there, to help them relate to their loved one, to help them do the things that they needed to do, or in the absence of a family, to play that role for the patient, so that no one would die alone.

People say to me, "Isn't that depressing?" I think in our society we're confused about definitions, and we somehow confuse depressing with sad. To be sad is not to be depressed. Seeing people die is terribly sad. It's incredibly sad. But it's not depressing. It's enlightening. It brings to you an understanding of life and of death, of spirituality, of the human condition, of intimacy, and love, and of being there for someone. So to me those deaths were an opportunity for someone like myself, who had not related to deaths in my own life that well, to do it well, to do it right. The goal of hospice is comfort. That's the goal. Only comfort. And to be able to fight for that person's right to die in comfort also gave you something very concrete to do to help the person.

One of the things about dealing with the dying and dealing with their families is that you become intimate very quickly. People tell you things and get close to you in a way that they don't at any other time in their lives. I found that while some of the families were the worst horrors you would ever want to meet, others were the finest examples of love and kindness. But everybody was dealing with shock and guilt. What was most moving to me were the mothers. Back at that time, a lot of the onus for why children were gay was put on the parents. The parents supposedly made their child gay — the mother was too dominant, the father was too distant, the mother dressed the boy in girls' clothes . . . there was always that kind of thing. I would watch these families search and search and search for the reason, and come to the realization that there wasn't anything to pin it on.

The risk of teenagers getting AIDS is probably the worst dilemma we deal with. I don't think we've yet found a way to impress upon teenagers that they're at risk. They say, "Look at what those adults are doing to scare us, and isn't that silly, and we don't have to listen to them, and you know how they exaggerate, and they're overemphasizing the case, and they're just trying to scare us, and that's not going to happen to us." We've not found a way to overcome that. We really truly haven't. I believe that as much education as we do about safe sex, kids don't hear it and don't think it applies to them, like that newspaper report about girls having sex with HIV-infected boys as a gang initiation rite. The girls said it was to show how tough they were. Not only were they tough enough to be able to take the risk, but they were tough enough not to get the disease. As if they could prevent it from happening by their sheer toughness.

I hope that many of us can look back to our own youth and remember what it was like. All that performance anxiety and both female and male macho of not wanting to be humiliated in your first sexual experiences, not wanting to look like you don't know what you're doing. And now besides everything else you gotta do, you gotta learn how to manipulate a condom, you're supposed to have that safe sex talk with your partner, and you don't admit to each other that it's going on — you just are so busy thinking, Will I do it right, how will I look, will I make a fool out of myself, am I going to humiliate myself? Am I going to look dumb, am I going to say the wrong thing, do the wrong thing? Talking about safe sex is just another added competency in a situation where you're feeling extraordinarily incompetent to begin with.

As the city's AIDS commissioner, I've been dealing recently with a real challenge from a group called the Coalition for Positive Sexuality, who in my estimation is saying, "We shouldn't be talking about choices not to have sex, because all kids have sex anyway, so we should just recognize that and help them toward personal enjoyment." As a public health official, you know, I really can't be concerned with personal pleasure. My job is to be concerned with public safety. In the public health department, our message goes primarily to kids that are freshmen in high school because the dropout rate in the Chicago public schools is 50 percent. Kids drop out when they turn sixteen. They turn sixteen, generally, when they're sophomores. So we only have one year to get them. So they're thirteen and fourteen, fifteen, and while it's fine to say, as does the Coalition, "Your sexuality and your orientation are terrific, and go out and discover it and have fun," the fact is that there are a lot more issues involved in sexuality than having sex. You need to have a level of maturity, you need to have a level of self-esteem, of self-understanding, of emotional stability, of spiritual growth, and of understanding other people in order to make choices about sex without being hurt.

I've heard a number of experts in adolescent education talk about all the influences upon teens. It's school and parents and peers and TV. I say, "Gee, that's really great, but the people that I'm dealing with have different external input from what you're talking about." They have drive-by shootings, they have a drug-addicted mother, they have no parent available, they have socio-economical problems, they fear for their lives, they're never going to get a job, so for us to come and talk about AIDS is like white noise. "How can I worry about something that's going to happen ten years from now when I'm afraid to walk from my building to the corner store because that gang that has the territory there will kill me?"

And many gay kids, even middle-class kids, are so disenfranchised in a different way. Maybe their mother isn't lying up in the bedroom on coke, but she's lying up in the bedroom denying that her kid is gay. God knows sexual issues aren't discussed enough in the home where heterosexuality is the norm, so they're certainly not going to discuss homosexuality, and that really leaves the kid on his or her own. That kind of abandonment, whether actual or perceived, leaves the kids to seek the very kinds of things that we're trying to have them look at from a more mature perspective: how do you get love, how do you get affection, how do you get attention? Your parents have abandoned you psychologically, if not physically, and one of the most feel-good wonderful ways to feel loved is physical intimacy. By not addressing their gayness in an open and fair fashion, we're leaving gay kids to seek gratification in a way that we would say is risky. If we don't give them reasonable ways to express their natural affection and love, such as walking hand in hand, kissing on the street, hugging, dancing cheek to cheek, frolicking on the beach, all of these things, we only leave them sex in a dark corner. The general population does not smile with understanding when they see a cuddly gay couple, no matter how old they are, but particularly when they're young. And if all gay kids are getting is negative messages, then they're not going to feel good about themselves, and it's hard when you don't feel good about yourself to say no, whether it be to sex or to drugs or to whatever.

Teaching about sex is tricky. Because you can scare kids with sex, too, if they think that they're going to be expected to do things they're not ready to do, or feel pressure to do what "everybody" does. You can't just hand a kid a pamphlet and a condom. You need to be there to answer their questions tomorrow, next month, six weeks from now. I don't like giving people condoms without showing them how to use them. I think of myself when I was a teenager, and if somebody put a manual in one of my hands and a condom in the other, and even though the manual had the instructions on how to use the condom, I'd be absolutely overwhelmed. So in our programs, we take the models or the cucumbers and show people how to put them on, and try it and get comfortable with it. I relate it very much to a girl who's coming into her period, and how much easier it is for the girl if her mother has already shown her the equipment, talked about tampons. Is it okay to use a tampon if you're a virgin? How do you insert it? What do you do with it? It's much more comfortable for young women when they've had a chance to see it, to touch it, to see how it works, to try it out, to make a mistake, etc., in the privacy of their own bathroom, before the event happens and here they are at school with blood on their skirt. I think about condoms in the same way, that it's so much better if you have a familiarity with the equipment before you're expected to use it.

I've been chastised a bit for publicly saying that I think kids need to have condoms demonstrated and given to them in sixth grade. Not because I want them to go out and have sex in the sixth grade, but I feel that if we want people to use condoms from the first time they have sex, then they need to know what a condom is and see it before the first sexual experience is upon them. And if they use a condom the first time, they're much more likely to use it every time. Although I'm a big promoter of talking to kids about the choice to be abstinent, I'm also a big promoter of giving the kids all the knowledge that they need, so that can make that choice in a way that's good for them and not because they're ignorant.

We can't be afraid to give kids information about sex. It shows our own insecurity about who we are. We're afraid that if we tell our kids about homosexuality they'll all go run off and be gay. That certainly says something very negative about being heterosexual, doesn't it? Everybody's not going to run off and be gay, everybody's not going to run off and have sex, everybody's not going to run off and be a punk skinhead just because they talked about it. I'm straight, but people have said to me, "Can you ever imagine yourself having sex with a woman?" Sure I can. Of course I can. I've been able to picture myself in a variety of situations that could happen, and they don't scare me. But some people think, If I think about it, I'll do it. Or something, I don't know. And they don't understand that the body is an instrument and if you play the instrument right, you get music out of it, and it really doesn't matter who the musician is if they know how to play the instrument. It's our psyche that takes over to say who we will allow that instrument to respond to, and the instrument itself doesn't know the difference. It's the psyche that knows, and that's what gives us our gender identity, and that's what gives us our sexual orientation, but the instrument is the instrument. And it's just who you want to do the playing. And you don't have to let everybody — or anybody — play your instrument if you don't want to.

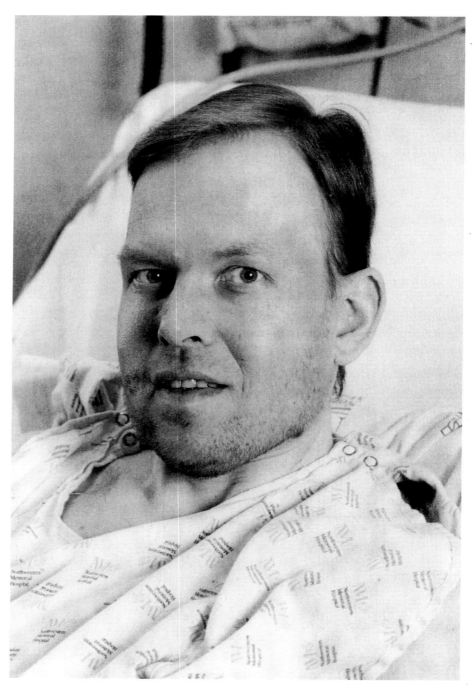

"Even in the gay community, there are people who have never talked to me again after finding out I have AIDS."

CHAPTER EIGHT

JUSSI KOIVUMAKI

Inevitably, discussion of AIDS permeates this book. The World Health Organization puts the number of people infected worldwide at at least 14 million, and although statistics tell us that the disease does not discriminate in terms of sexual orientation, it has, like nothing else, had a defining impact on the gay community. It has killed many of us, and at the same time has been a rallying force for unity and political action. Benefits for AIDS organizations, as well as memorial services and funerals, are, ironic and sad to say, part of the fabric of gay social life. Everyone knows people (or is a person) at various stages of the disease: this friend, this lover, is HIV-positive, that one was in the hospital but is doing much better, that other one is nearing the end. Jussi Koivumaki, who first came to the United States from his native Finland as a high school exchange student, then settled here in 1980, first believed in 1986 that he might have been exposed to AIDS. Since then, it has been a part of his life.

I made a trip back to see my family in Finland three years ago, and my goal for the trip was to tell my parents that yes, I have AIDS. My family at this point already knew I was gay, and that they had dealt with quite well. But I was going home to tell them yes, I have AIDS, but look! I'm doing wonderfully, I'm healthy, no problems. As it happened, I was rolled out of the airplane in a wheelchair. I got so sick, I ended up spending three weeks in the hospital. I almost died. I had an intestinal infection that went into my bloodstream. I went septic — I had three different kinds of bacteria in my bloodstream that are only supposed to be in your intestines and they were all over my body. Got pneumonia on top of it all, and I was unconscious for over a week and eventually just slowly, very slowly came out of it.

I first thought I might have AIDS about eight years ago, when I was talking to my ex-lover Skip on the phone one night, just after I had left him and moved to Chicago. I didn't even have a phone yet, so I was calling from a pay phone, and that's when he told me he had just been diagnosed with AIDS. It was a cold, nasty night, and I had to go back to my terrible studio apartment to try and figure out what was going to happen. I knew that if he had AIDS, the chances were fairly high that I would come down with it. At the time I wasn't really aware of how AIDS was spread, but I knew that since I had lived with him and we had had sex that I probably would have AIDS myself.

A little over four years ago, I was diagnosed with full-blown AIDS. I got pneumonia, and they didn't know what was causing it, whether it was bacterial, viral, or whatever. The diagnosis was "etiology unknown," and my T-cell count had plummeted down to about 220, and at that time you were diagnosed with AIDS if your T-cell count was under a certain amount. The doctor told me, "You have AIDS." It didn't come as a surprise, but it shook me up and woke me up, and I realized that it was time to get back on track.

I had always felt that there was a definite plan in my life for me. And when I started veering a little bit too far from the road that I'm supposed to travel, something would happen that would push me back in the right direction, like when I was younger and doing an immense amount of drugs that almost killed me. That really scared the hell out of me, but it made me straighten out my life. And being diagnosed with AIDS was again this force that kind of pushed me back into the direction that I was supposed to be going. I had been working as a bartender, making lots of money, but also drinking too much, going out too much, and generally not doing anything productive with my life. I sat down and took account of where I was, what was I doing, what it was that I wanted to do, and what I needed to do to get there. It was a real slap in the face: "You're not immortal; you are not going to live forever." It wasn't easy because I had to give up this fast life and start taking stock of what I was doing, and it wasn't pretty because I realized that I hadn't accomplished anything. I'm sure it's one of these crises that everybody goes through; I just happened to go through it earlier because of AIDS. I had had some goals at times, but they were always fairly short-term, within a year or two. And even though now my goals are short-term, I know that I'm going the right way. I'm at least going in the right direction.

I went back to school, to study sound engineering and video production. Music was something that had always been close to me. I grew up in a very musical family — music was a big, important part of our family, one of the few things that really brought us together. And so I felt that this maybe was the direction for me to go. So I started as a sound engineering major, but as time went by, I realized I was more of a visual person, and I saw music as pictures, I saw books as pictures and as movies and as videos. I started my own production company in the beginning of this year called Me Too Productions. Me Too is my nickname, given to me by my friend Michael several years back. When I went out with him and his friends, I found it a lot easier when we ordered dinner just to get what someone else was ordering: "Oh, me too." And it kind of stuck. Me Too Productions — I'm the only person in the company at this point — makes short video features on gay and lesbian issues. I did one documentary on same-sex marriage, following a couple through the whole process of getting married during the big gay rights march in Washington in 1993. I want to let people know through my work that we are out there — we are all around, and we are your neighbors, nieces, nephews — we're just there. Because once people realize how many of us there are and how we are all around and that we are everyday people, it makes it a lot easier for us to be accepted as a community and as people and to be part of the whole culture.

I've also gotten involved in this organization called Direct Aid, which offers monetary help to people with AIDS who have kind of fallen into the cracks. We give money to people with AIDS who need food, or their rent or utility bills paid. When you're "out" about having AIDS, people often ask what organizations you feel are doing the most. And I usually say Direct Aid. Because we don't get government grants, we don't have grant writers who are getting paid to write applications for grants or anything like that, and we are trying to keep it as a grass-

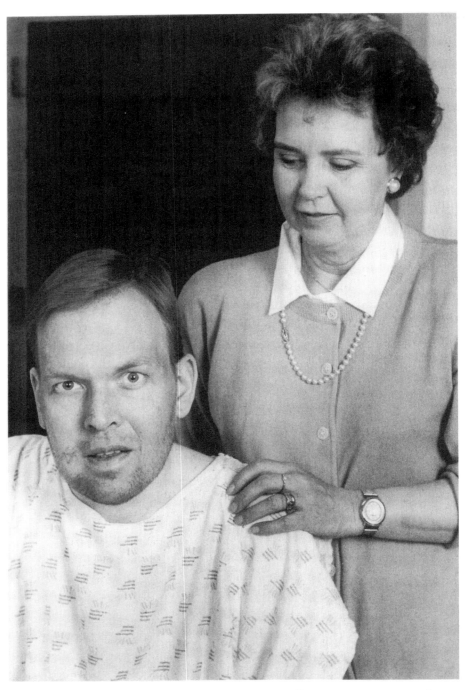

Shortly after our interview, Jussi became ill once again. Here he is in the hospital with his mother, visiting from Helsinki.

roots organization without growing into this incredible conglomerate where you start spending 75 percent of your dollar just to run the organization.

You don't — you can't — think about having AIDS all the time. You think, Yeah, it's there, especially when things get rough, when I get sick. For about the last three weeks, for example, I've been experiencing this explosive diarrhea. Among other things it's really embarrassing and puts me in awkward situations at times, and while you can laugh about it afterwards, when it's happening, it's not very funny. But things like that are always there to remind me that, hey, make sure you stay focused on goals and things that you should be doing. About a year ago, I was in this situation where a few projects that I had been working on all came to an end at once. I had no goals, I wasn't focused on anything, and all of a sudden, I got really sick. I ended up in the hospital for a week or so, with a really bad intestinal infection. That's when I realized I had to keep my projects overlapping so there's no abrupt end to everything all of a sudden that's just going to leave me sitting there with noplace to go. I have to have something planned ahead, so there's continuity, something that will keep me focused, keep me going, give me a reason to go on. That's one of the lessons I have learned in the last year or so.

I'm not bitter about having AIDS at all. I'm doing the best I can to live with it and deal with it. I *am* bitter about the fact that even today, after years of this disease, there is not enough information out there about how to avoid getting AIDS. I feel that the United States government has been despicably absent from AIDS education. And even in the gay community, a lot of people won't deal with it. Some people are just hoping that if they don't see the elephant in the living room, it's not there. They'll just work around it and say, "What elephant?" And that's scary. I'm not angry about *having* AIDS. I don't feel that it has been a curse or anything else, although there are days when you spend half a day in the bathroom and you feel kind of frustrated. It's frustrating, yeah, but it's the lack of education that angers me.

I had never thought of myself as an activist before. I was just a bartender — I was a person who worked in a gay bar and my friends were gay, I was gay, but I never thought of myself as political or anything else. I took this gay and lesbian literature class in college, and I discovered that most of the students in the class, who were about ten years younger than myself, thought of me as a "militant homosexual" because I felt so strongly about being out. The school said that if we wanted, they were willing to change the name of the class in the transcript to "Special Topics in Literature." And I said, "No, it should not be changed. If you are out enough to take Gay and Lesbian Literature, then you should be out enough to be able to admit you took it." I am gay, I am HIV-positive, I have AIDS, and I feel that it's important to be out about these things because if you don't tell people what your medical status is, you reinforce the same kind of fear of people with HIV as there has been of people who are gay. Even in the gay community, there are people who have never talked to me again after finding out that I have AIDS. They're afraid to deal with it.

I feel it's important not only to be out, but to let people know that, yeah, you can live with AIDS. I don't know how long I'll be doing it. There are people who have lived with HIV for more than ten years, ever since doctors were able to diagnose it. I may be one of those people; I may not. And on the other hand, I may not die of AIDS — I may die in a plane crash while going home to Finland tomorrow.

I definitely do get scared. I'm not really scared of dying — everybody always thinks of AIDS as a death sentence. Well, we all are going to die. There's this song by the Eurythmics, something like, "I'm not afraid of dying; it's living that scares me to death." I'm afraid of not being able to do all the things I need to do, whatever they are. I still don't know everything I'm supposed to do. I'm afraid of pain; I'm very afraid that infections or the virus will affect my brain and make me lose my control, lose focus, and not be able to keep on doing the things I want to do. I've seen so many of my friends die. I have buried fifteen friends in the last four years, one of them my ex-lover. Skip passed away four years ago. He was forty-one when he died. But it's interesting, hopeful, that most of my friends didn't die bitter, didn't die being angry. I just try to believe that when it comes my time to die, I will have completed what I'm supposed to do. It's that belief that keeps me from getting freaked out and just running down the street and screaming, "Aaugh, I can't deal with this." My life is like a set of lessons that I'm supposed to learn, and because I didn't learn my lesson of making the most of my life at first when I got involved in drugs and all that, something had to come along and teach that lesson to me again — and make sure now that I'm trying to stay on the right track. Because I don't think I can afford another lesson. [Laughs.] I don't think I want to come back and do this all over again.

"We're not talking about being discriminated against because of something we do. We're being discriminated against because of who we are."

CHAPTER NINE

ARTHUR JOHNSTON

There have been several stages in gay and lesbian civil rights activism in this country. As Renee Hanover describes in chapter 12, much of the fight in the '50s and '60s was for protection from police entrapment and government investigation. Gay men and lesbians thirty years ago would not have fought, for example, for domestic-partner benefits or explicit inclusion of gays in statewide antidiscrimination laws. Gay was a code word, not something you saw splashed across the screen on a news broadcast. But the late '60s brought "gay pride" and a resurgence of feminism, and the early '80s brought the AIDS crisis, all of which coalesced gays and lesbians into a group determined to exercise political force. "These are basic civil rights — there's nothing special about this stuff," says Arthur Johnston, a political activist and the owner, with his lover, Pepin, of a popular gay video bar. Art is currently working to add sexual orientation to the classes (such as race, sex, and religion) protected under Illinois statewide antidiscrimination laws.

Gay people are the new communists. With communism dead, extreme rightists and others need to have an issue to organize around, and we're it. They perceive us to be an easy target. There are biblical things they can say about us. They have proven that they can raise funds talking about us. And with the rallying cry of traditional families and family values, they can use us that way. I think they've proven the amount of money they can raise is quite remarkable. There has to be a devil, and we are it. Communism was the devil, but communism doesn't exist much anymore as a threat, and we fit all the old kind of conspiracy theories because we are everywhere, here in your own homes, your towns. We're the easiest group to hate.

I think I knew I was gay long before I knew the word. My earliest recollection is when I was eight or nine years old, I was attracted to men and preferred to be around men. Acting on those impulses is another matter — that didn't happen until much later in life, but I've always known. I knew when I was in Cub Scouts; I knew when I was in Boy Scouts. And I always sensed that it was somehow something that society at large didn't approve of. Nobody made me gay. I was always gay; I knew it. I knew intuitively that most other children I knew were not. I think children have amazing radar about these kinds of matters. And I knew it was something I needed to keep hidden. Things are a little better for kids now, but it's still a very complicated, difficult thing. Going through puberty is the most complicated, wrenching experience for anyone, even if your sense of self, even if your impulses, even if your biological changes and all those things seem to be exactly in line with what all of the rest of the world is doing. Let alone when you have the sense that you are different. It's a horrible time.

I grew up in a small industrial town north of Buffalo, New York, a place called North Tonawanda. And I knew nobody. I simply knew no one who was gay — no one in my own family, no one among the children I grew up with, no one in my school. I truly felt that I was the only gay person. I mean, I knew I *couldn't* be the *only* one — it just didn't make sense to be that different — but I didn't know anybody else who was. There was a boy who lived nearby who liked to secretly put on dresses and things, but that was not my sense of who I was. I was far too naive to understand that there were many kinds of gay people — that there are gay people who look like lumberjacks, gay people who look like ballerinas, and there are gay people who look like Wall Street lawyers, that there are gay people who look like everything — and this boy who liked to dress up in frilly clothes was kind of frightening to me. I suppose I was hoping I wasn't like him, because I could sense that he also liked men. I thought, Well, he's different and I'm different, but we're not different in the same way.

All kids need role models. It's horrible growing up and not having anybody you can look to who you think you could aspire to be. I certainly looked: I looked to sports people, I looked to politicians, I looked to leaders, and there was nobody anywhere that I thought I could be. The result was that I didn't believe I had a future. I couldn't be a fireman, a policeman, a teacher, an *anything,* because I didn't know any gay people who were those things.

I met Pepin, the great love of my life, in 1973, and we've been together ever since. We had this opportunity with a friend who wanted to open what he called a video bar, and this was 1981, when we didn't know what *video* meant. The friend unfortunately passed away soon after the bar opened, so somehow I turned from a high school teacher into a bar owner and manager. Today there are places, some but not enough, for young people to meet and talk to other young people who are struggling with what it means to be gay. We have sports leagues, we have clubs and choirs, churches and neighborhoods. We have these things. We didn't have those things for a very long time. For gay men, and to maybe a lesser extent for lesbians, bars were all we had. People would go to bars not just to drink, not just to pick somebody up, but because that was the only place they could go and be around other people who you felt were somewhat like yourself.

Gay and lesbian bars and bar owners have long been active financial supporters of community causes, and in the mid-1980s there was growing frustration that Chicago did not have any antidiscrimination protection for gays and lesbians. There was a movement to force the city council to call up a bill, which had been sitting around for about sixteen years, that would outlaw discrimination. Some people planned a rally the evening before or maybe a couple of days before the vote. And somebody had proposed that all the bars should close on that Sunday evening in order to promote the rally. I was asked to come to meetings to talk about this, and I said, "You know, if you can show me how closing the bars is going to get more people at the rally, then I'm all in favor of it, but I don't see a connection; what you're going to do is alienate business people who have traditionally been very supportive." So I suggested that instead of doing that, why didn't we keep the bars open and use the bars as staging locations for buses? Have buses come, pick people up at the bars, and take them to the rally? Well, of course, we all know the danger of suggesting something, because then we get to do it.

So I called all the bars, and everybody was generous, everyone gave some money, and the small, the very small bars that were barely making it, we asked them for less or we made sure someone would subsidize their share so that we could say that every lesbian and gay bar in this city put up the money to arrange buses. The bars provided enough money to not only run a number of buses to the bars, but also to use those buses to pick up people — this is Sunday, now — at religious services. The buses picked up people at the Dignity meeting, which is a Catholic gay group, at the Metropolitan Community Church service, and a variety of others. We made a very strategic decision that we would not rent from a private company, but from the CTA, the Chicago Transit Authority, getting the same kind of buses that come and go every day on the streets of the city. We thought it would be significant in terms of our proving to people that it's our city, too. I don't remember now whether there were eight or ten buses, but there were plenty of them — full Chicago public transit buses, pulling up and encircling City Hall, and opening up the doors, all of these gays and lesbians. It was the first time for many people they'd ever been on a bus with only other gays and lesbians. And to see these buses pulling up and unloading people and the crowd more than double in size when the buses arrived was an electric moment. "It's our city, too."

That whole experience energized me. I saw that things can change. We didn't expect to win the vote, and we lost, but it was a crucial slap that our community needed to feel. Most people who went down to the voting session had never been to City Hall, didn't even know where it was or how it worked. We packed the galleries with our people, and we listened, we heard the terrible things being said about us. We heard about being damned to hell, and people were very disturbed, very shaken up, very hurt in many cases. But angry: we don't accept victim status anymore.

When any person cannot be who that person is, cannot be true to his or her own self publicly, it is demeaning to his or her existence. That's one thing. But the lack of equal protection also means a person can be fired from his or her job simply because the employer thinks that person is gay or lesbian. And this happens every day. There are documented cases after cases after cases of someone being fired from a job because a coworker was jealous, or office politics, or whatever, and spreads the rumor that somebody is gay or lesbian, and the person gets fired for it. There are no legal recourses for that, except in the nine states that have passed this legislation — nine out of fifty — and in many of the large cities, and small cities and municipalities, often college towns and so on across the country. If you don't happen to live in one of those places, you can lose your job, you can be denied an apartment, you can be denied a promotion. We're talking about discrimination in employment, in housing, and in credit transactions. And in public accommodation. Public accommodations is something as simple as being served in a restaurant, or renting a hall for a party, being treated fairly on buses, trains, etc.

These are basic civil rights. "Special rights" is the buzzword used by our opponents. There's nothing special about this stuff. It's not special rights to be able to sit down in a restaurant and not worry that maybe you've smiled too much at the person of the same sex at the table with you. We have reports all the time of restaurants saying, "You're not our kind. Get out of here — we won't serve you." Many of our more conservative gays and lesbians seem to feel that Well, it can't happen to me because I'm not extravagant, I don't wear an earring, I don't talk about Judy Garland movies. The problem here is that we are not discriminated against because of something we say or something we do; we are discriminated against because of who we are. Joe Steffan was thrown out of the Naval Academy not because of something he had done, but simply because he's a gay man. The guy who was thrown off the bridge and murdered in Maine was not thrown off the bridge because he'd been caught in a homosexual act. He was thrown off the bridge because he was perceived to be a faggot. Of course, it's already illegal to kill somebody, but here's the point: where discrimination is allowed to exist, violence flourishes. The increase of violent attacks against gays and lesbians that happened in Colorado after Amendment 2 was passed is direct evidence of what we're talking about here. So we must have these basic antidiscrimination laws in order to achieve our simple equal status in society. Whether gays and lesbians are 10 percent of the population or 4 percent or 12 percent really doesn't matter to me. How much discrimination does there have to be before you say that's too much discrimination? Isn't one case of someone being discriminated against enough for there not to be discrimination? And if anyone is discriminated against, everyone is in danger.

You achieve rights by passing laws, and you pass those laws by finding out how the process works, whichever legislature you're working in. You look at numbers and you see what's involved. There's an old cliché that says that anybody will say yes to any question if it's asked by the right person. So you find out who the right person is. And if the person who needs to be there talking to this particular legislator is a six-foot-ten drag queen, then we will find a six-foot-ten drag queen. If it's a five-foot-four lipstick lesbian, then that's what we'll find. We will find whatever it takes to get that yes vote. In Chicago, a very Catholic city, we use nuns. These aldermen would suddenly become like little children putting out their hands to be slapped, you know: "Yes, sister." The nuns would simply ask them to vote for this legislation and would talk about it and were incredibly helpful.

I always have a one-item agenda. And at the moment that is basic antidiscrimination laws to protect gays, lesbians, and bisexual people on the basis of sexual orientation in the state of Illinois. That's what I'm doing now. Will there be other items that will take my attention after this is done? Absolutely. But in my experience the only way you accomplish things is not to have a fourteen-point or eighteen-point or twenty-point agenda, because then you can't go forward. When I am working on AIDS funding, that's my whole agenda and I don't want to talk about anything else. Because there are legislators who will support AIDS funding who would not, right now anyway, support basic civil rights for gays and lesbians. Others might feel the opposite way. The moment you go into a legislator's office and talk about civil rights *and* AIDS funding *and* abortion funding *and* domestic partnership, you lose. The moment you demand that your supporters on any one issue all support you on five or six other issues, you get nothing. When you have too many litmus tests, you simply don't get anything done.

You need a certain number of votes to pass a piece of legislation, and you have to go where the votes are. Even though gay rights have traditionally been seen on Democratic platforms, if the votes you don't yet have are in the Republican party, then you lobby the Republican party. We must believe that our issues are strong enough and deserving enough and that we ourselves are smart enough to figure out how to get votes from both parties. One thing that's fascinating about human

Art addressing a business organization of gays and lesbians

rights issues is that they always, if we handle them correctly, cross party and ideological lines. And that's what it must be. Because human rights, civil rights, must cut across all those boundaries.

Maybe someday we'll actually have federal protection, but I think it's still a little ways down the road. The folks who go to Washington, D.C., the senators and the representatives, will need to come from places where this legislation has already passed. The old saw that politics is all local is absolutely true. No senator or representative is going to get to Washington and have his or her mind changed on these issues there. It has to be done at home, in Joliet or Kankakee or Sioux City or Sacramento or wherever. That's the only way it's going to happen. There are really three arenas where we can win. One is city, county, and state initiatives that support gay rights, the second is in courts, and the third is the election of qualified openly lesbian and gay officials. Those are the areas where we're going to win.

CHAPTER TEN

FRED AND DANNEL MITCHELL

With all the progress in society's acceptance of gays and lesbians, a family like the Mitchells is still mighty rare. Dannel says that the parents of other gay kids he knows "were ready to put them in a mental ward and were screaming at them and beating them," and the testimony of the other young people in this book, as well as the stories related by youth workers Jerri Lynn Fields and Michael Cornicelli, bear him out. Parents' reactions to many things — friends, goals, accomplishments — matter to kids, and what is perhaps most remarkable about this father and son is their acceptance that Dannel's sexual orientation is a matter of fact, not a matter of choice.

DANNEL: Last summer, I started finding out more about myself, and slowly but surely I started telling my mother that I thought I was gay. It really wasn't hard to tell her because we've always been close, ever since I was young. So when I told her, she wasn't really shocked, because she said she always knew but didn't really want to realize it. In her heart. Basically, my whole family knew. They had seen it in me as a child. When I told my dad, he said he always knew, too, because even though I don't act real flamboyant, I had different ways as a child and all — I always clean up and cook dinner and cook breakfast — and they said they kind of seen those ways in me and they thought it would just be a phase or something. But I didn't grow out of it. My whole family knew, but they didn't want to deal with it.

MR. MITCHELL: I had the impression for a long time that Dannel was gay. It didn't surprise me, like he said. The only effect it had on me was

"If my son's going to be gay, I'm going to accept it. Doesn't mean I have to like it, which I don't, but I will accept it."

that I just didn't like it. But I accepted it because I knew it was coming for a long time.

I was raised up the old-fashioned way, and I know society frowns on homosexuality, but this being the '90s and me knowing how things have changed, my only concern is his welfare and his well-being. If he's going to be gay, I'm going to accept it. Doesn't mean I have to like it, which I don't, but I will accept it, and I will do whatever I can to make sure that he follows the right path. My saying is, If you're going to be gay, be the best there is. Know about it. Understand that there are communities where you can go and live comfortably and be who you want to be. But where we live now, it is better for his safety and well-being not to stand up and shout it from the mountaintop to everybody, because they're not going to accept it and they're going to want to hurt him.

DANNEL: And so we looked in the newspaper and other places to try to find a place to help me understand myself, to get help so I can deal with society and the way they talk about me, and so we stumbled upon a group for gay teens. I went, and they taught me a lot of stuff about AIDS and things. They helped me better myself, to be more cautious and more protected out here from different people, cruel people.

The first time I went, I was very nervous and everyone was sitting around, and I was like, well, I was kind of scared to say the word *gay*, because I really didn't know these people. I really didn't know too much about the group — I just knew it was a gay and lesbian thing. But I was just so afraid to mention the word *gay*. And so I was nudging this one girl, "What's going on? Is this, like, for gays and lesbians?" I was just so scared to say the word. And she said, "Yeah," and I kind of relaxed because everyone opened their arms to me, and it got to where I felt welcome. And it was nice, it was really nice, because I met people that had the same feelings I had.

I think people are born gay. I can remember, even when I was five or six, saying, "I see that guy right there; he's cute." I really didn't know too much about love and all this other stuff, because I was young, but I could see myself looking at the females and only liking them as friends, and the guys, I had crushes on them. I can remember this one teacher, I had a real big crush on him, and I had crushes on some of the male students in my school, too. But females, I just never romantically or sexually liked them.

I can remember in sixth grade having a crush on this eighth-grade boy, and although a lot of girls were hitting on me, I didn't get turned on by them. I like girls mentally, but I just can't think of them romantically. At school I associate with girls because I feel that I have a lot in common with them, whereas with the boys, some of them, it's hard to talk to them when you have a crush on one of them.

It's very hard at school. A lot of people talk about me because I'm smart and, you know, I act different from the whole crowd at my school. My mother says it's just out of jealousy and some people just don't like me. Some of my friends at school know about me, but I generally only talk about it with my real close friend, Latasha. She tells me things about her, and I tell her things about me. I told her I was gay, and she wasn't shocked, but she asked all kinds of questions. She was curious, and I tried to answer her questions because I didn't want her to be ignorant about gay people. We're real, real close, and she wouldn't tell anybody. I think there are other gay kids in my school, but it's just so hard to point them out, because they all hide behind the stereotype of acting manly. I'm sure there are a lot of gay people at mostly every high school. I go to an all-African-American school, and everybody there has that stereotype, you know, "Don't act like a faggot." Boys are supposed to be boys, and girls are supposed to be girls. So if there are any other gays or lesbians there, I'm sure they're keeping themselves in the closet.

MR. MITCHELL: See, Dannel has chosen something that's not accepted by the normal standards of the world. I know what he's going to have to fight. I don't want to bash my race, but black people can be very volatile about people who don't fit in. Especially gays. But I want to try to at least be in his corner.

DANNEL: I definitely want to go to college, and I was thinking about psychology and sociology because I know I'm gay and I want to know why people are who they are, why they act the way they do. Since I'm good in science and biology, I thought about becoming a doctor, but I also think about becoming an actor or a model. I really crave the public

eye for some reason. I really want to tell people about gay people. You don't have to accept us, but just know that we're here and learn more about us so when you see us, you won't, you know, talk about us. My dad is giving me money for tuition at this place called ETA, a theater center for African-Americans where they offer acting classes and put on productions, and I hope it will be a great place for me. Actors know how to adapt to different things. If you want to be an actor, you have to learn how to adapt because you have to become the person that script tells you to become. And so I believe if they know how to do that, then they know how to adapt to a person who's different from them.

I'm hoping I'll meet my companion in college. Not inside a bar or something like that, but in college. That way I know that he's going after what he wants. I think about going to Northwestern — that's a really nice college. Because it's close to home but it's far from home.

MR. MITCHELL: I think the reason why he's choosing Northwestern is he has a friend who's gay that goes there. I'm going to sit down and talk to him: when you choose a college, choose a college for what it's worth, not just because you've got a friend there. Of course it's good to have friends or somebody you know in college, because college is a scary place. But you got all kinds of colleges to choose from; at almost any college you're going to find a gay community.

DANNEL: I went up to Northwestern, and it's nice, it's really nice up there in Evanston. And you know, this is the kind of place where I would like to be. And Chris is there, but by the time I get there, he'll be graduated. Chris is out to everybody in his dorm. I can see the way they accept him; he'll say hi, and they won't just be, like, "Hi" — they'll say, "Hey, Chris. What's up?" and they'll get to talking, and everybody in his dorm likes him for *who* he is, not *what* he is.

What I'm looking for is somebody very intelligent, with money, someone I can always talk to, come to him with my problems, and we can talk about things. I don't want our relationship to be based just on sex. I want our relationship to be based on going places, nice places, traveling, enjoying things together. We both have to be intelligent and have money. Because money isn't everything, but it's nice.

MR. MITCHELL: I sit and listen to him talk, and he always manages to stick money in there. Sometimes I think it plays a major role in his choices. I really do. I'm the one that pushes him to say that education is a big key no matter what you want to achieve in life. Money comes second. I'm glad now that he's finally following some of the things that I said to him, because I used to say, "Show me the motivation, that this is what you want to do." Because I've felt sometimes that he wasn't really motivated. He'd want to start something and he'd get so close to it, and then he'd drop it. But with him coming out and saying he's gay, I really see the motivation working.

When he meets somebody he really wants to be with, and I can see that the guy is positive and beneficial for him, I won't have a problem with it. I would treat it just like Dannel was my daughter, bringing home a first boyfriend. Yes, I'm going to be full of questions, and I'm going to have opinions, and I'll probably jump to conclusions, but I'll just have to sit back and say to myself, "You went through the same thing when you were young and met someone special. You had to go to the house and deal with the dad."

His mother tried to pull a little shock therapy on him the other night, using religion: "If you're gay, you're going to go to hell," you know. It shook him up a bit, and they had a good little cry-fest. And I've seen both sides of the coin as far as that goes. I'm old-fashioned when it comes to how I was raised, but I'm also a modern-day man because I know how society has changed. And how values have changed. If you live your life however you choose, regardless of what some standards of religion say, just be true to your belief. I used to go to this African-American church where the majority of people in it were gay. I learned just from being around them, and I've seen their up sides and their downs. I just lost my youngest brother to AIDS. He also attended the church. He was married, had two kids, but now I come to find out that maybe he had a sexual relationship with somebody who was affiliated with the church because there was a lot of that going on back then. He might have been gay, might have. We all just didn't get into each other's personal lives. At one point in time even my youngest sister thought that I might have been gay because I tended to stay by myself and didn't have a girlfriend or anything. She didn't know I was just footloose and fancy-free.

DANNEL: Sometimes my dad preaching at me gets to me and I don't like it, but I know he's telling me the truth, and so I try to listen. I always listen, but sometimes, you know, it's "Y'all be finished — I want to watch television." I know that I am really fortunate because I have parents who understand me, and when I told them I was gay, they didn't want to kick me out of the house. Because most of my friends tell me that when they told their parents, they were ready to put them in a mental ward and were screaming at them and beating them and I think I was — am — really fortunate. The hardest part about growing up gay is getting people to accept you. Because if you don't have anybody accepting you or loving you, that's your life right there. You maybe can make it here alone, but you'll be so lonely, and lonely leads up to depression, and depression leads up to suicide. You need acceptance.

MR. MITCHELL: What I really want for Dannel is for him to find a place where he can get an education, where he can get some positive motivation, as if to say, Okay, you're gay — let's get on with your life. Let's not get hung up on what the world is going to think. Take what you are and make it work to the best of your abilities. This is what I really want for him. I can't ask for anything else.

CHAPTER ELEVEN

CAROL SADTLER AND JACKIE TAYLOR

Heather Has Two Mommies, *a picture book about a girl with lesbian parents, was a cause célèbre throughout the early 1990s. According to the Intellectual Freedom Office of the American Library Association, it was one of the most frequently challenged titles in school and public libraries in 1993. While "family values" spokespeople were waving the book around as evidence of the perversion of traditional morality, gays and lesbians quietly continued having, adopting, and raising children. The Sadtler-Taylor household, far from being a den of iniquity, would be recognizable to any family with small children, and my interview with Jackie and Carol was punctuated with naptime noises coming through the baby-alert intercom. The children, Lucy and Grace, were still quite young when we talked, and Carol and Jackie know that they will all face a new set of circumstances when the girls start school and otherwise begin to move outside the family circle. "We'll be there for 'em," says Jackie, and I felt that this confident couple was up to the challenge.*

CAROL: I had never really wanted kids. And then, when I was approaching my forty-first birthday, it just hit me one day: Are you really going to pass this up? I was watching a little baby in an airport, and I saw clearly that I was going to have to do something like this now or just pass it up forever. There's something about turning forty that makes you start evaluating these things. I think it happens in spite of yourself. So I had been on my way to meet Jackie, and when I saw her, I said, "Let's talk about having some kids."

"Our children are going to grow up in a home where difference is valued."—Jackie (at left)

JACKIE: What Carol *really* said was, "What would you think if I told you that I wanted to have a baby?" And I said, "I would be thrilled, but don't talk to me about it till you make up your mind. I don't even want to entertain the thought unless you're sure." I had always wanted children — all my life I wanted children. I never imagined I wouldn't have children, never. But when I was married, we had a fertility problem, and we had three failed pregnancies. That just broke my heart. Even after I came out as a lesbian nine years ago, I still wanted children, but I didn't really see that it was possible at the time. I don't know if I thought so much that there was a conflict between being gay and having children, but I was in this volatile and not particularly healthy relationship where it wouldn't really have been an option. And when I got together with Carol seven and a half years ago, she just wasn't interested in having children. Carol knew I really wanted children, and she would always say, "If you really really want to do it more than anything, then you should, and we'll just figure out a way because I don't want to stand between you and your heart's desire." And I said, "No, because you would resent it and we would break up, and I really want to be with you." It felt to me like it was a loss I would always live with. So when Carol told me she wanted to think about it, I wanted her to be sure. But practically right away she was saying, "Oh, but I really think I do want to do it." There were a couple of weeks where she was still saying that officially the status was "thinking about it," but I think she pretty well had made up her mind.

So then we had to decide *how* to have babies. Given my history, I knew I wasn't going to get pregnant. Since I figured I couldn't even get pregnant when I had a husband handy, no way was I going to attempt it again at the age of thirty-eight. So the big question was would Carol get pregnant or would we adopt? We kicked that around for about a month. Carol decided she didn't really want to get pregnant at her age, and she also felt like there were a lot of children who needed homes. But it was a funny month, because during that month we were sizing up every male we knew as a possible sperm donor. I was looking at guys I hardly knew thinking, Hmmm, no glasses, good eyesight — or does he wear contacts? Stuff like that. Going through every possible male that we knew at all, considering the logistics of what would he think if we asked him to donate sperm, talking about all the pros and cons of a known donor or an unknown donor and what kind of relationship you could have with the person, on and on and on. And then we said, let's just adopt.

We began to do research on how to adopt, and we quickly found out that in order to adopt infants, we were probably talking about an international adoption, either that or a private adoption. We started going to different adoption agencies and hearing their spiel and finding out what countries would deal with single women and trying to get a line on what agencies might be willing to work with us and sort of not probe further into our living arrangement.

For the first adoption, Lucy's, we were working through an agency here in Illinois, and they gave us a referral to another agency, which then gave us a referral to the attorney in Peru. And when they had a baby, they called, and we went down. For the second adoption, we called the attorney in Lima, and when they had a baby ready, they called back.

CAROL: That makes it sound a lot simpler than it is, of course, because you have an extensive screening process here, and then there are long court proceedings in Lima.

JACKIE: After the process here, each adoption took about nine weeks in Peru. You get the babies within twenty-four hours of arriving, but you have to wait for all these bureaucratic things: appearing in court, going to the police station, getting a psychological exam, getting fingerprinted, going to Interpol. And all this time you're down there taking care of a baby in a foreign country, and living in an apartment — or in Carol's case it was in a hostel.

We had to do each adoption singly because in Illinois it hadn't happened yet that a lesbian couple was allowed to adopt as a couple. We each did one of the adoptions as a single parent, and we were very careful about not revealing our status as lesbians while we were in the midst of the adoption process because we were concerned that we wouldn't be able to adopt. If we didn't have trouble here, we would almost certainly have trouble in Peru. We were very lucky. It was February when I first filled out an application to the agency, and by July 8, Lucy was in our arms. It was really hard because we were doing this charade of being a single mother and her friend, and Carol was in the room, but they were handing the baby to me, saying, "Here you are, Mom — now you're a mom."

CAROL: I had to sit like a spinster aunt or something, you know?

JACKIE: And we had to pretend it was a much more important moment for me than for Carol. It was uncomfortable for me every time they called me "Mom" to think about how Carol was feeling.

My parents came down to be with me as well. They had been very dismayed when they first learned that I was a lesbian, but over time they have responded as well as I could ever hope. My father's a Baptist preacher, so it wasn't really in their hopes and dreams for me that I would be a lesbian. They think it's a sin that we're lesbians, but they acknowledge my freedom as an adult to choose my life without them commenting on it. They're very supportive of Carol and my relationship. Very. They really love her, and they know what a wonderful person she is. I was nervous about telling them that we'd decided to adopt because I didn't know what they'd think. But they said, "Oh, Jackie, we're so glad you finally figured out a way to be a mother." I said, "Well, I was kind of nervous about telling you." And they said, "Why?" and I said, "Oh, I don't know, I thought maybe two lesbian mothers might give you pause." They said, "We think you and Carol will be wonderful mothers."

CAROL: They're great, they really are. My parents weren't very supportive at all, initially, and they were just a little bit too silent about it for my own comfort. But we went ahead anyway, and by the time Gracie came along, my mom was down in Peru with me.

JACKIE: She spent four weeks down there with Carol; she was a real lifesaver.

CAROL: She was there getting up with Grace at night so I could have a chance to sleep; she did the shopping and cooked every meal.

Lucy is thrilled to have two mothers. In fact she thinks she has a lot more than two because she's very close to the baby-sitter and we have one or two friends that spend a lot of time over here. If I have to go on a business trip or something, Lucy will start calling the baby-sitter her Mama D. She calls us Mommy Jackie and Mommy Carol; she also calls us Jackie and Carol. And she also calls us Mother, Mom, Jacqueline, Carol Ann. She knows the power of names. She talks about having two mothers a lot. She says, "Me and Gracie have Mama Jackie and Mama Carol."

JACKIE: When we're both home, she'll say, "My two mommies are here. One mommy is cooking supper, and the other mommy is changing out of her work clothes." She knows that there is such a thing as daddies, but she hasn't wondered where hers is yet. She knows her friend Alex has one mommy and no daddy, but I don't think she's noticed that it's different yet. I think over time each one of the girls has developed a very important mother-daughter relationship with the "other mother."

CAROL: We've done quite a bit of reading in adoption books about the kinds of questions kids ask, the kind of grief the other kids give them, the sense of loss they're probably going to have about their birth families, and so on. So I don't think I'm kidding myself about those difficulties, but I think if they go into those things feeling really happy about themselves they're really going to be able to handle it. There may be a time — probably there *will* be a time — when they resent us and resent their situation, and maybe when something goes wrong, they'll say, "Why couldn't I have had a family like everybody else?" That's going to hurt all of us, and it's going to be hard, but I think that we have a really good start.

JACKIE: I wish it was possible to keep them from being hurt in their lives, and I know that it's not. I know that kids can be really cruel to each other, and with these girls there's a lot of potential things to be cruel to them about, lesbian mothers being only one. Being adopted is another, and their ethnicity still another, and God knows what else. There's no way to get through childhood without encountering the cruelty of other children. You could say, well, by being lesbians we're one source of the difficulty, but I think it also gives us a strength: we've lived with difference and we've lived with being outsiders and we've thought a lot about what that means. It's changed the way that we relate to everybody, not just gay and lesbian people. So the girls are going to grow up in a home where difference is valued and the reality of homophobia and racism and sexism and all that is not covered up. There'll be at least some context for understanding what's going on and thinking about what kind of world we'd like to have instead of the one we're in.

This whole neighborhood is Mom, Dad, and the kids, except for a couple of divorced mothers, I think, and some older people. It really is a very traditional neighborhood. And everybody is fine to us. Everybody knows Lucy and Gracie; everybody was excited when the kids came to live here. It's a block where there's a lot of spirit. We have a big block party and people know who everybody is. We were on the radio last year as lesbian moms, and somebody in the next block down heard it, so probably somebody on this block heard it or talked to somebody who heard it, too. I'm sure that everybody knows, plus we've had two different baby-sitters from across the street, and they'll see books in our home that are lesbian this or gay that. And there's a king-size bed in our bedroom.

CAROL: But nobody's mother says, "You can't baby-sit for them." I'm sure they're curious. I know. I used to snoop when I baby-sat for people.

JACKIE: The whole neighborhood must know that not only does it look like we're lesbians but that we *are* lesbians. The man next door is the sweetest, sweetest neighbor, and he's been really dear to us from day one. The summer before last, his son died of AIDS, and then I felt like I understood why he was especially nice to us, that he felt a family connection. He once said something that specifically addressed the fact that the girls had lesbian moms, something like, "Well, they're going to have a lot to deal with when they go to school." And we said, "Yeah, they will, but we'll be there for 'em."

CAROL: I just think the more people talk about these things, the more you start to realize that somebody has a gay nephew or son or daughter or maybe a best friend who has gay children — the more people talk about it, the more it's not a secret, the more you realize that a lot of people either know somebody or are somebody.

JACKIE: I just pretend that homophobia is over. I treat people as if they're going to be pleased to know us and think our family is wonderful and be happy for us, and so far most people can do that. We really

Jackie, Carol, Grace, and Lucy

want the girls to know a lot of different kinds of people, and more men than we have in our lives right now. Grace really loves men.

CAROL: Grace practically stands on her head for the men who come over here.

JACKIE: Yeah. And Lucy always has to get everybody's gender straight — we have one lesbian friend who's quite butch, and whenever she comes by, Lucy will say, "She's a man? She's a woman."

CAROL: She said this summer that she wanted to be a motorcycle guy when she grew up. There's a bunch of guys in the alley who work on motorcycles, and Lucy's fascinated.

JACKIE: One day we were talking about who was a man, who was a guy, and she said, "I'm a guy," and I said, "I don't think so," and she said, "Yes, motorcycle guy." I said, "Oh, well, you can be a motorcycle woman." So now she's going to think that we want her to ride a motorcycle! I'd rather she didn't, but if she must, I'd rather she did it as a woman than a man.

We know there will be troubles down the road. We anticipate that there will be some period — every lesbian we know with kids has encountered this — when the girls will be embarrassed about the situation. We figure there might be a period where they want to say they don't have two moms, they have one mom. And if they want to say that one of us is their aunt and one's their mother, or one is their mother and one's their mother's friend, we're not going to fight them. Because we feel like they don't have to fight our battles, and they don't have to be as out as we are, and we have to respect what they need to do about it.

CAROL: It's real interesting when you think about the possibilities of two women or two men rather than a man and a woman raising kids, because it can be less dependent on traditional sex roles. That's the thing that I've always loved about gay relationships. There aren't tracks for them — you invent the possibilities as you go along, and you're not limited by roles. I think it's equally exciting for this whole family thing. You're freer.

JACKIE: I really feel like the girls are their own, they belong to themselves, and that our job is just to give them enough room and enough structure so that they can flourish. In a way, not knowing a lot of details about their biological heritage has been kind of liberating to me, because I don't say to myself, "Well, you come from a long line of people who know how to do X" or who have this or that capacity —

CAROL: Or "Oh, you're just like your grandfather."

JACKIE: When one of them likes spicy food, we say, "Oh, she gets that from Grandma Taylor," or when one of them can't go to sleep at night, we say, "Oh, she gets that from me." But it's always said with a sense of humor; it's always a joke. They come from a fascinating country and have a wonderful heritage, but we don't know any details, so it's totally up for grabs. I don't know if they have inherited the musical genius of a Mozart or not. And I don't know if they are descended from incredible athletes or people who like to sit. It just becomes a question of giving them room to develop whatever gifts they have. I don't know how to say it well, but it's a nice feeling to me and it feels like a new kind of family. I really don't believe I'm invested in having these girls turn out to be carbon copies of me. I truly and honestly do not care what their sexual orientation might be or what sort of families they'll build of their own. I hope that they'll be able to have some kind of friendship/family network as adults, and that they'll be able to hold jobs and take care of themselves. If they can do that, I'll feel like we've done our job as parents. We don't care if they want to buy big cars and we don't care if they want to go to the prom; all that is fine. We do want them to have some concern beyond themselves.

CHAPTER TWELVE

RENEE HANOVER

Art Johnston, interviewed earlier in the book, says of Renee Hanover, "She's a street fighter, that one," and the tone in his voice conveys equal parts exasperation and admiration. Now in her sixties, Renee (pronounced "Reenie") came to Chicago from New York with her then-husband in 1950, sent by the Communist Party to influence workers and unions. At that time, being a communist — like being a homosexual — could get you put in jail, so Renee's work was, as she puts it, "underground." As a political organizer and later as a lawyer, Renee was involved in civil rights work and other social justice movements. Her discovery, after her marriage had ended, of her own lesbianism also led her to the legal defense of homosexuals arrested for what was called "public indecency," which could be anything from loitering in a public restroom to being caught in a raid in a gay bar. In the 1950s and early 1960s, lawyers such as Renee and organizations such as the Mattachine Society and the Daughters of Bilitis worked quietly for homosexual self-acceptance, public understanding, and for the right to be free from government harassment. The same concerns face gays and lesbians today, but the strategies are much more political and visible. While much honored in the gay and lesbian community for her pioneering work, Renee is adamant that she doesn't belong to any one community; instead, she says, "It's all connected."

I wanted to be a civil rights lawyer or perhaps a labor lawyer. But when I had four months to graduate from law school, the dean called me in and told me that he had been informed I was a lesbian and I was suspended from school. I finally got back in and graduated, but at the time it was a very tough thing to deal with. And if that wasn't enough, my lover killed herself. She was really the first contact I had, not only sexually, but intellectually, friendwise, anything to do with being a lesbian,

"Back in the 1950s, suicide was very common among lesbians. That was the way to handle being a lesbian."

and she was a dynamo. So it was then that I was determined that no-body else could do that again. Back in the 1950s, suicide was very common among lesbians. That was the way to handle being a lesbian. It was almost like the AIDS plague, where you would hear news of so-and-so dying, so-and-so taking her life. The attitude was that it was all understandable. Too bad that she wasn't strong enough, but we could understand why she did it — that was the attitude. It was really very sad; you certainly felt like an outlaw. And I certainly felt like one in terms of being of a religious minority. After the Rosenbergs were electrocuted, being Jewish wasn't too safe, never has been, and this was soon after the Holocaust. Being gay or lesbian wasn't the safest thing to be either. But it's interesting that the internal family pressure that a lot of these women were getting was the worst of all. My lover's mother used to call her "it," meaning she wasn't a he, she wasn't a she.

I knew about ten lesbian women at that time, and a lot of them had gay male friends. If they went to dinner or the ballet or the opera or the theater, a lesbian couple would go with a male couple so that it would be seen as two straight couples double-dating. Although there were a lot of gay men that were known in the area, we really all felt we were the only lesbians around. I remember somebody saying something like "I think there's a lesbian that lives on the North Side." And everybody laughed at her. We certainly didn't think there were any lesbians who lived outside our lesbian circle. And these were women who had master's degrees; most of them came in from out of town to go to the university. They were bright enough, but they were not political. And none of them was Jewish, and for a while I just thought lesbianism was a Christian thing. I did eventually meet a young Jewish woman who was a lesbian. She later burned herself to death.

In those days, you were either butch or femme. I remember that I sure as hell wasn't going to be femme, because I considered that I'd been femme all the time I was married. But on the other hand, it was very hard for me to play the butch role, especially since I'm five feet tall and my first two lovers were over six feet. You can't feel very butch in those situations! What I found out was the femmes were the stronger ones in so many ways. Now they think of femme-butch as emulating the straight community, but I don't see it that way at all. We had no role models, we had nothing to go by, and, besides, there were femme-butch relationships of different degrees.

It wasn't so much that the butches wore pants and the femmes wore dresses — it was the hairdos. The femmes were wearing bouffants. I remember this one blonde — I mean, blondes to me were as foreign as anything could be. The femmes wore long hair and bouffants, very high on their heads, or pageboys, which was like some popular actress at the time. You were mostly judged by your hair. There was a bar in the city here that's still open that wouldn't serve me a drink because I wasn't really an authentic butch, but on top of that I was political. That was horrible. I was a danger to everybody — it was guilt by association, you know.

I had been a student and, later, law associate of Pearl Hart. She was one of the founding members of the National Lawyer's Guild, which was a left-leaning lawyers group. She was a very good lawyer, she was very pro-labor, and she was a role model for a lot of people. And she did pro bono work for good causes. If you get a chance to just walk around this neighborhood and cross the street with any woman, say, maybe eighty and over, they would know who she is. The local gay and lesbian library, the Gerber-Hart library, is partly named after her. I was in the library one day when an elderly woman walked in, and she wanted to know if the Hart library was named after anybody in Pearl's family, so I came over and I talked to her, and she told me Pearl Hart had been her lawyer. I photocopied a picture that was in the files there of Pearl and gave it to her. The way she held it — like she was going home to frame it — you could tell she was just so thrilled. Pearl represented gays also, but her feeling was it's nobody's business what you do in your own bedroom and you shouldn't tell anybody that you were gay or lesbian. And of course looking at her, she wore very manly clothes, and that was one thing that she was totally unaware of, that everybody knew she was a lesbian. She was a fantastic lawyer. I remember her walking into the courtroom while another case was going on and the judge said, "Good morning, Miss Hart, it's an honor to have you in my courtroom. What case do you have?" And he interrupted the other trial to call Pearl's case — she was defending a gay man — and after the state put on its case, the judge said to Pearl, "Do you have any suggestions to make about this case?" And she said, "Yes, your honor, I would suggest this case be dismissed." He took her suggestion. I said to her, "You've been teaching criminal procedure? I know what your criminal procedure is. You walk in there and you overwhelm them!"

I'm probably the only woman in Chicago who knew the insides of every men's washroom in Lincoln Park. Lincoln Park spreads from the North Shore to the South Shore, and gay men used it as a cruising place. Gay men were into anonymous sex at the time. They would go into the washrooms and stand over the urinals next to other men and indicate that they were interested in having sex. Police would arrest them for public indecency, which was either self-masturbation or mutual masturbation, things like that, so the police department used to have policemen hide in broom closets in these public washrooms. They had quotas for arrests so that they could get points for the sergeant's exam. We have captains now, commanders now, in the police department, who won their positions on the backs of gay men. They would try to get a good-looking policeman to pretend that he was gay and entrap gay men into making advances. Sometimes they would arrest gay men simply because they were there and they needed people for their quota. I don't think they were doing that to straight couples. I mean, there were straight people who were having sex all over the place, too. The only thing that's holding back straight guys are women. And women aren't too good at holding back anymore, either.

I took a lot of these so-called "indecency" cases. I was just operating from the basic rights of an individual and thought these people were being harassed terribly. I represented quite a few military people up at the Great Lakes Navy base who had been in 'Nam and they had five months to go on their enlistment and were being shooed out as gays because the Navy could save money that way, didn't have to pay them a pension or anything like that. And golly, I remember one time something like forty-seven of them were arrested and up for charges. I went up to the base to see them because the last thing I needed was forty-seven Navy people in my office. I've always been a pacifist. It seemed like the whole Navy to me. So I went up there to see them at Great Lakes, and it was hard to get their attention at first because they were talking about "we" and "them," claiming that they weren't gay, they were straight, and so forth and so on. I finally said, "Look, fellas, I'm a lesbian and you're as queer as I am, so let's get that straight with the 'we' and the 'them.'" I couldn't get them quiet for ten minutes — they were hootin' and hollerin' and carrying on. And by the way, that was probably the basic reason that I came out as much as I did. It wasn't so much as a political statement but mainly to put aside this nonsense of pretending.

The women's movement in the 1970s helped me in a lot of ways because when I came out as an open lesbian, a lot of my friends from the early days were terrified of being with me. I was the first openly lesbian lawyer in the United States, and my friends felt it was social, certainly professional, suicide. It wasn't until the women's movement made it easier for lesbians to be a bit more militant and to identify themselves in a very positive way that I regained my friends. I had five very lonely years, certainly lonelier than when I was underground, because when I was underground, I had communist friends.

It's all connected. During the Vietnam War, I was doing counseling and keeping an eye on the military. There are gay men now who when they recognize me on the street say, "Oh, you're Mrs. Hanover, aren't you?" And I say yes. "Oh, you saved my life." I say, "Oh, I'm glad about that." Turns out usually that I got them out of the military. I was the old lady in any movement that developed. You're never the right age. I have an affinity with teenagers who have ideas of their own. You're never the right age, is what I want to tell them. So don't wait. You're never the right age for people, you never have the right politics for some people, so you have to start developing your politics now, your instincts now. You need to realize that racism is poison, classism is the worst, and that every time they want to separate you from somebody, and by "they" I mean the powers that be, they're doing it to hurt you. I don't care about gays in the military. I don't want *anybody* to be in the military. I think the gays in the military are apolitical, that they're going to go along, they're going to be brainwashed. It's a volun-

Renee in 1968

teer army now — these are young people who can't get a job because of the economy. They feel that they can get an education in the military; they feel that this is security for them. They go into the military. Well, I think a gay person who can tolerate the military is already lost. I saw on a television show a gay man who was kicked out of the FBI, and he wants us all to support him to get back in. The man has to be crazy. God knows how many anti-gay things he's been involved in. Gay men are enticed too easily; they're too close to the pie. To get their piece, gay white men need only to be treated like straight men. They're just one step away.

The greatest militancy that we're seeing in our community now is from groups like ACT-UP and Queer Nation. And this is because these people are facing the inevitable. They're ill; they're dying. Deaths of close friends in the lesbian community because of cancer, in the gay community because of AIDS, have been overwhelming to me. Absolutely overwhelming. All I can think of is all these young people dying. I've written wills for some of the guys who've since died, and I remember them saying, "Well, we want you to be our executor," and I'd say, "Oh, no, you need to find somebody around your age, and I'll be long gone," but they're gone and I'm still here. It's only when fellows like Larry Kramer and the rest of them say, "Look, the government doesn't give a damn that we're dying and doesn't want to spend the money on research, doesn't want to give us drugs that are needed" that people get a glimmer of how the government's going to behave toward them. And yet the movement is saying, "Let's become part of the government — oh, we're tight with the president, we're close, we're getting in now." But what will they do when they get in?

It sounds very dramatic now, but when my husband and I were sent by the Communist Party to Chicago those many years ago, we were given a half-dollar bill that was to be matched with another half-dollar bill somebody here would have, and that would be the proper contact. I'd forgotten about it until just a few years ago, when my family and I were celebrating Passover, a holiday that commemorates a time of oppression, just like we have now. One of the things that you do at the Passover seder is break a matzoh in half, hide one half, and have the children go look for it and bring it back to the table. Before the ceremony can continue, you have to match that half to the one that you have at the table to see that it definitely is the half of the whole that you broke. For some reason I was intent on seeing that it was the correct piece and trying to match it, and I saw the similarity to my own story. The Passover seder is a seder for freedom, and when I held that half-dollar bill long ago, I really felt that I was on the same sort of mission. I might be slowing down a bit, but I still do.

"Even now, I'm afraid, being a foreigner, that I might be deported." — Joe

CHAPTER THIRTEEN

JOE AND CHARLIE

Being out is not an absolute condition. You can be out to your friends, for example, but not to your parents. Or maybe you've told your parents, but you haven't told your boss. Joe and Charlie (these are pseudonyms) have several reasons for choosing to lay low about their sexual orientation and their relationship. Joe is afraid he could lose his green card, which permits him to work in the United States. Charlie is apprehensive about the possibility of his family's rejection and about being harassed or even losing his job. Both men, though, buck old stereotypes of "living in the shadows," or other such metaphors for closeted life passed down to us from the pulp novels of the 1950s. They live together, travel together, and have a wide circle of gay friends. They seem anything but furtive in building a life challenged not only by heterosexual mores but by conventional thinking about the problems of interracial and intergenerational relationships — Joe is white, and seventeen years older than Charlie, who is African-American. At the time of the interview, both men were reconsidering their decision to remain closeted, contemplating coming out and "letting the chips fall where they may," as Charlie puts it. That's not an easy decision, and it's one that most gays and lesbians confront over and over again as they pass through various stages of life.

CHARLIE: In my family, it was just unheard of to be gay. The religious aspect was probably the most difficult to overcome. I was in college the first time I had sex with a man, and after, I thought I was going to go to hell. Nobody in my family was like this — why was I different from everyone else? By the time everyone else in my family was twenty-five, they were married and had kids. I had always thought I would find a wife in college, and by the time I was forty my children would be twenty years old. And I would still be young and active and enjoy my children when they were teenagers and take them to ball games and

103

stuff like that. After I did have sex with a man, I said to myself, Oh, goodness, am I really going to go to hell for this? But the more it happened, the more I sought it out. There was a reason I kept doing it. It was the first time I had opened up and was sexual and really let go. It felt very nice.

My family doesn't discuss it. Joe and I have been been living together two years and dating for two before that — I don't think there's been a weekend we haven't been together since the first time we met. Joe comes over for family functions; he's almost like a part of the family. They like him. They know he's my roommate. Before we officially moved in together, I was always over here anyway. My family would ask, "Why aren't you ever at home?" I presume that they might think I'm gay; I've thought about bringing it up, but then on the other hand I —

JOE: I think they know.

CHARLIE: I think they know, but I have to get up the courage to say it. What's hard is when certain subjects come up and then I don't say anything. Most topics, I'll always open my mouth. The hardest time was when Magic Johnson was diagnosed as being HIV-positive. I kept thinking, Well, he's a basketball player and he's straight, and there's a certain amount of treatment that he's getting, a respect that he's getting, that people who have been dying for many years haven't gotten. When my family would talk about AIDS, I would think, Well, they're not being fair. They're not understanding. I kept thinking, This could happen to me. Would they say the same thing if it happened to me? As a gay male I should say something. But what if they say something real negative or conservative and it hurts? You think, this is my brother, this is my sister, and this is my mother. I love them, but I see that they're kind of closed-minded. And it hurts, so you kind of don't want to say anything.

JOE: I know Charlie's family likes me, and I think they're very nice people. But I don't think they know what to do with me. It may be the fact that I'm foreign, might have something to do with the fact that I'm white, might be because I'm gay.

I was brought up in Ireland with three sisters. Neither of my parents finished high school, but they're very open-minded people. I only heard them once make a remark about any group of people who were different. My father didn't like the English too much, but that's understandable.

My first sexual experience was when I was twenty-three, I guess. I came out kind of late. A lot of it had to do with growing up in Ireland, which was a very repressive place, and in the Catholic church, to be gay was to be, you know — one of the tribe of Sodom and Gomorrah, hellfire and brimstone and all that. By the time I was about eighteen, I had really lost my respect for the church. I enjoyed growing up in Ireland very much; it's a beautiful place and a wonderful place for a young person. A chance to be out in nature all the time, and I played lots of sports, and swam, and bicycled, and hiked in the mountains. But by the time I was entering my twenties, I knew I had to leave.

I went to London, where I came out with a bang. I was out every night till three in the morning. It was the late '60s. That's in fact where I met Americans for the first time. It was a very good time to be gay there. You'd go home with somebody for the night, and you had nice, friendly, affectionate sex, and even though you knew the next day you wouldn't see them again, they'd cook you breakfast or you'd cook them breakfast. It was very affectionate.

I still had a lot of religious struggles. It wasn't actually till my early thirties that I finally got rid of any fear about going to hell. But I would have to say I'm still very angry — Charlie knows I'm always going off at the Catholic church for the long history of repression of gay people. I was brought up Catholic, but later on as I got to know people from other churches and read history, I found that Christian churches collectively have been very oppressive toward gay people. There's no evidence in Christian scholarship, in biblical scholarship, that there's anything wrong with being gay, but that idea is still perpetuated. I guess what distresses me as a human being is that no matter where you look, so many people are being oppressed. Women, gays, children, blacks in this country, all over, the world is a mess, human beings are a mess. Charlie's always telling me to shut up, but I'm on my favorite soapbox.

CHARLIE: It's one of the areas where we have a lot of lively discussions and Joe's much more angry about it than I am. Much more. I see the same problems, but I just feel like it will eat you up inside if you focus on it. I do get angry at things I see on TV, and Joe'll say, "Well, maybe you're getting too angry." I'm black and I'm gay, and being gay I think is worse, in terms of how most people feel.

JOE: Because everybody hates gay people: blacks, white people, Mexicans —

CHARLIE: I was brought up being told that there was nothing wrong with being black. You didn't need anyone to validate that; you just realized it was true. But for being gay, I didn't get that same kind of self-esteem. I had to develop it, and it's not like you just one day say, "I'm gay, and I have all the self-esteem in the world." It's a long process. You don't have your family to support you. And then there's going to bars. Joe says he met a lot of nice people that way, but I don't think my experiences were as nice, where I actually felt good about myself. Sometimes I would meet someone and go home with them, and I would say to myself, This is a mistake. Sometimes I would say, Oh, my goodness, I've just wasted five hours in a bar, and the only thing I can show for it is the loss of twenty dollars. It was new ground, no rules, no experiences to go from.

JOE: The options, though, were pretty poor — unless you were very, very courageous and open, which most people weren't and most people aren't, the only places you were allowed to meet people were in bars. There's tremendous pressure on gay people in bars. And people often drink because they get nervous, and then sometimes you don't make smart decisions.

CHARLIE: The more I kept going out, the more I thought that this is a pattern that's happening over and over again. And I'm not meeting anybody. On the occasions I did meet somebody, did it make up for all the time where I didn't meet someone, someone nice? I kept thinking there has to be another way to meet men. Joe and I met in a bar, and I'm not ashamed of it. For that one night, the bar served its purpose. But we told my family that we met in the gym. Because that would be the only plausible place where they could see Joe and me meeting: he's not an accountant and I don't work in a university, but my family knows we both work out, so we said we met at the gym.

JOE: That's what I told my family, too. Because my family doesn't know I'm gay either. I'm going to see my family in a while, and Charlie's coming with me. He's met my sisters; they came over for a visit, and they in fact invited him before I actually said he's coming along. My family wonders why I left Ireland, and my mother even asked one of my Irish friends why — she thought they might have done something to me. I don't think they realize why. But when I get back from the trip, I'm going to write to my sisters and tell them. They may already know — I don't know. They're very nice people, and I like them a lot, and they're very open. Ireland's changing now — there are a lot of changes, thanks be to goodness. It'll be interesting — I suspect they'll be very supportive. Even my mother might. This friend of mine said that I should go ahead and tell her; she thinks my mother is much stronger than I give her credit for. But at this point, would it do any good? She'd probably say fifty novenas every day. My friends say I'm being paranoid. And maybe so, but I'm too afraid to take the chance — it's too much of a chance for me.

Even now, I'm afraid, being a foreigner, that I might be deported. There was a famous case in Texas only a few years ago where this English gay guy opened a business and employed forty or fifty Americans, and then some of the neighbors reported him to immigration. He took it to court, but he lost and was eventually deported. I forget his name, but it was in the gay papers for a long time. On the immigration forms somewhere it says that the two things that barred you were being a homosexual or communist. It's probably unfounded at this point, but I'm still somewhat fearful that if I went public, I might be deported. What if there was a religious backlash against a book like this and Patrick Buchanan and people like that got on the road and starting digging and witch hunting? The McCarthy era seems like a fairy tale today, but I could see it happening again. And I wouldn't go back because I couldn't get a job, and I don't have enough money to retire, so all my worlds would be cut off. I'd be destitute if I were deported. I'd be too ashamed to go back to my family, not having any money.

CHARLIE: You have to think about the backlash. My ambition is to get a better job than accounting and to be financially secure. And I think,

Well, if people know I'm gay, will that prevent me from advancement? You don't come out at work, at least not where I work. I work with a lot of sexist men. It makes me nervous.

JOE: Two people who used to work for me engaged in extremely hateful behavior when I was inadvertently outed by a friend. He sent me a copy of the *Advocate,* a gay magazine, through interoffice mail. It was in an envelope left on my desk, and these people opened it, and the cat was out of the bag. I was their supervisor and was leaning on them at the time (because they were lazy SOBs), so they used it against me. They put AIDS warnings on my door and some other really nasty stuff. I was very proud of myself, because I didn't do anything. I stuck to my guns, and eventually they quit. I felt I won, but the toll was very high, emotionally and psychologically. It was a very difficult two years.

CHARLIE: I listen to Joe when he tells me about that, and I say, "I don't want to go through that."

JOE: So much is taken for granted by straights. They don't understand what it means not to be able to walk down the street and hold your lover's hand, not to sit in a restaurant and look romantically across the table, that you *have* to go to gay places to feel that comfortable, or else you have to be truly ballsy. Most of us don't have that kind of courage. The price tag is just too high.

CHARLIE: People just assume that gays are like the gay men and the lesbian women they see on TV or in some movie. They don't know that I'm somebody's brother and that a lesbian woman is someone's sister, and we're just like everyone else. The older I get, the less concerned I am about other people finding out. I think if Joe didn't have a problem with it, I'd say, Let's be out, and let the chips fall where they may. Something happened to a friend of mine just the other day that bothered me. This guy is ill, he's dying, he's had AIDS ever since I met him, but now he's getting progressively worse. He told his mother about himself a week ago. He called his mother and told her that he was gay and that he was HIV-positive. What if that happened to me and I had to tell my mother and she had had no idea?

CHAPTER FOURTEEN

MARTA

Most gay and lesbian teens are afraid to tell their families, and many, as Marta points out below, have good reason to be afraid. Even the most sympathetic family may think you need a psychiatrist (as Jeff Rivera's did); others may forthrightly reject you. Marta (a pseudonym) is still trying to make peace with her family but seems to have found a way to hang on. Some kids don't — soon after I met Marta, she called late one cold Friday night to ask if I could help a friend of hers, who had been thrown out of his house because he was gay, find a place to stay. In making phone calls to homeless shelters and runaway hotlines, I discovered that it is very difficult for someone under eighteen to find refuge without the intervention of the police — a scary prospect for someone suddenly without a home. There is also the prospect of being without a life. Although research studies conflict on the percentage of gay teens who commit or attempt to commit suicide (one study contends that gay teens are three times as likely as straight teens to attempt to take their own lives), actual numbers seem beside the point when it is you, as it was Marta, who find yourself facing despair.

I've always known that I'm gay. It's so hard for people to believe unless, you know, you yourself have gone through it — "How can you be four years old and know that? How can you even know what it feels like to like someone?" But you just do. You feel different. I grew up in Guatemala, and I knew that I just liked being with girls. And I liked girls. As young as I was, I wasn't ignorant about that. I knew I liked them, but they always teased me about the fact that I never liked dresses — I can't remember a time when I've liked dresses. Everybody used to tease me about it, and I hated it. I had to wear dresses, but I felt awkward — I didn't feel right. I guess that's where I developed my theory that you should let people do what they want as long as they're not hurting you or hurting anyone else. I'm not going to criticize people, because I've been criticized and I know I don't like it. I think I've learned through that.

I think I must have been about five years old when I had a crush on my eight-year-old neighbor. It's hard for people to understand because they think, Hold on a second, you were only five years old — how would you know? But I did, and when I left Guatemala, I was sad because I thought that I would never see this person again.

I met my friend Cathy in sixth grade. She was my friend, but I knew I "liked" her from the beginning. We have such a special friendship, one of those friendships that can't be torn apart — you know, when you've gone through the impossible together. In eighth grade I decided to come out, and she was the first person I told. She was just the most understanding person that I've ever met and said, "Yeah, that's okay." She comforted me, and the one thing she didn't do was turn me away. Even though she might have felt a little bit awkward, she never turned me away. And then the summer before my freshman year, I decided to tell her that I liked her, you know, romantically.

I told her on the phone. I said, "I really love you," and she's like, "Yeah, I know." "No, Cathy, I really love you, okay?" And she says, "Wait, hold on a second, what do you mean?" So I say, "I've always liked you, I like you now, and I love you." I remember that right after I hung up, I was sitting in bed and pulled the sheets over my head, thinking, Why did I do that? That was just the stupidest thing I've ever done. But it never seemed to affect her, so we just kept on being friends. We went through stages. First she knows I'm gay, and then we get used to that. And then she knows that I like her, and we get used to that. I've told her, "I like you, but first of all I'm your friend." I'm always backing her up no matter what. When she had a problem with her boyfriend, I helped her. I remember when she became sexually active for the first time, it bothered me a lot, but I told her, "I just want you to be safe. You know if you ever need anything from me, tell me." That was really hard for me. But like before, we got used to that.

Then I met this other girl — her name is Jennifer — and we went on a date. She asked me out, so I said to Cathy, "Cathy, I'm a little worried, how about if I can't kiss right?" I said, "Why don't you just teach me? Why don't you just teach me so I'll do it right?" And she's like, "Okay, fine." But we're joking and I didn't expect anything to come of it. I remember we were going to the library to study for our finals, but we had to stop over at my house. And I say, "Why don't you just teach me now?" That was the first time we kissed. But she's straight and she has a boyfriend. She tells me she does like me more than a friend, but then she goes, "I want a family. I want kids." And I can't give her that. It's hard for me, because I'm so close and very far. That's how we are now, I guess. Sometimes she has a hard time because she's always with me and I think people have asked her, "Are you a lesbian?" And I feel it's because of me.

My parents were divorced before I was born, and I've moved around a lot. I lived for a while with my mom out west, then with my dad, even for a while with a teacher. When I was in fifth, sixth grade, I lived with my aunt, and we used to argue so much; there were so many fights. I was always crying, and I knew it was because I was gay and I couldn't say it. I remember we used to have fights about how I dressed. One time I told her, "You don't understand me. If you could just understand me, then we wouldn't be fighting." She said, "What? What's the problem?" It was one of those times where you want to say something so much but can't. I just kept saying, "You don't understand." And that was always the big fight. And I knew it was because I was gay but she didn't know that, so she thought I was just defying her. I didn't tell her until sophomore year.

In junior high I was extremely suicidal. I had so many problems that sometimes I really didn't see a way out. I sat in my room in the dark and cried. I knew that if I couldn't come out, I didn't want to live. One day I got really upset and went down to the basement and just cried all day and listened to my favorite tape, and I was going to end it all. But I thought, No, I can't do this. I don't believe in suicide. I think that when people try to kill themselves, they're supposedly killing the bad things — they don't have to deal with the negative things anymore — but you also kill the good things. My personal belief is you don't have the right to take your own life. And I always got the feeling that things would get better. It doesn't always seem like that, but they do. I look back now, and I can see I'm better off than I was. And if I would have given up then, I never would have had the chance to be here now. People always tell you that, but you don't believe it until you see it for yourself.

I moved in with my dad after things didn't work out in another place I was living. It was not the best alternative, but it was something. He has four kids and his wife, so it's a family. He was always referring to me as the spoiled apple — he had to watch out for me because if he didn't, I would spoil all the other apples. But I like my half brothers and sisters. That was part of the reason I wanted to move in. And I was really tired of moving.

I wanted to come out, but I didn't think it was wise for me just to say it out and out, so instead, I started giving off little hints, you know. That girl I told you about, Jennifer, lived next door. It was a minor attraction, no big deal, but we were always together, we were always talking, so they started getting suspicious. Then last Christmas I was with my brother and my stepmom, and she gave us something to drink, some alcohol. We were just talking, and I started talking about Jennifer. And I started talking about the way I felt about Jennifer. Being drunk was an excuse to say something, to clue them in about what was going on with me. I decided that if they confronted me with it, I wasn't going to deny it. That was my way of coming out.

My brothers are okay with it, especially my younger brother. But my two little sisters reacted differently, and the one who's twelve gave me a real hard time. She kept saying, "Yuck. How am I going to tell my friends that I have a sister who's a lesbian?" My stepmom and my dad heard this, and I guess it bothered them. They didn't want to say anything to me, but they weren't real happy about it. My dad pulled me aside one day and said, "You know, I understand you. I know about these things. I've met other lesbians; I've even lived with some of them. All I ask is that you keep it out of the family. I'm not condemning you, but it's not something we want in the house." So for a long while, for a couple months, it was there, but it was never talked about. My dad's fear was that people would find out. That was the big main thing.

One night Cathy called me, and I knew my dad was listening on the other line. We were having this really intense conversation, and she made a comment about our relationship, and I took such a long time to respond, you know? I heard my dad coming up the stairs, and I said, "I gotta go." And he comes in my room and says, "I want to talk to you *right now*." I'm like, "Ooops." He was *really* upset. He says, "You think I'm stupid or something? I'm a man and this is my family, and you're disgracing it." He was upset about what Cathy had said, and he slapped me. I stood up, and he threw me down again. And I stood up, and he threw me down — we did this about five times. Until I decided for my own health, for my welfare, I'd better calm down. I just let him talk; I just let him scream. Then I got up and said, "You know what? I'm leaving." He says, "Fine with me. I'm ashamed of you. Your father died — your dad is dead for you. You don't have a father anymore. Because I'm ashamed of you." So I think, Well, I guess my dad did die a couple of minutes ago. So I left.

I went to live with my aunt again. She really surprised me, you know? She said, "I don't care what people say — I love you for whatever you are. All I ask from you is to please go to school and get a career. Get ahead. If anybody has a problem with it, then they can go to hell." I don't think she's really crazy about me being gay — she's not — it's not something she's totally accepted, but she tells me it's my business. I'd lived with her before for seven years, basically from third grade to freshman year in high school, so it's like a whole life. She saw me grow up. She was like my mother for a long time. But we were having so many problems. I recently told her, "You know what? You see all the problems we had? It was because of this. Because I couldn't tell you about me."

Being gay is not something to be argued about. This is why my family has had such a hard time. It's something they felt had to be argued. No, it doesn't. It's not an argument. It is something that *is*. No matter what you say or do, it's not going to change. It's hard for me to accept that my dad kicked me out. I think that's going to stay with me for the rest of my life. Because I know now I'm not going to ever talk to him again. He doesn't want to speak to me. It's been three months since I left.

My main thing is to finish school. I have one more year to go, and I definitely want to go to college. I think what I really want to do is help kids like me. Not necessarily gay kids, but kids who have problems. Because I was never allowed to be a kid, never. I always had problems that adults gave me, and I didn't know how to handle them. I had to learn how to handle them. I think kids should just be kids, and there are times they need people to help them out. Why should a fifteen-year-old be worried about where they're going to live? Or where they're going to be going to school, or *if* they're going to go to school? It's too much. I remember I used to sit down and try to do my homework and I couldn't stop thinking, What am I going to do? I just had another fight with my aunt, she's not happy with me, she wants to send me to my mother, I don't want to go, and I'm trying to do math here at the same time. People won't believe me when I tell them that I know about life. "You're just a kid — you don't know what you're talking about. You've just started living." I don't think so. I think I know a lot.

CHAPTER FIFTEEN

THE REVEREND DR. JOHN SCOTT

Can you be gay and a good Christian at the same time? Despite what many TV preachers tell us, there is no unity of thought on this question. The Metropolitan Community Church, for example was founded specifically as a Christian ministry to the gay and lesbian community. Even in denominations where the practice of homosexuality is condemned as a sin (Roman Catholicism, for example), there are groups and individuals working to change official thought. Dignity and AGLO are two such groups in the Catholic Church; Integrity is a similar organization in the Episcopalian Church. In Judaism, as well, there are varying degrees of tolerance — Or Chadash is a gay and lesbian Jewish congregation in Chicago, but they meet in a Unitarian church! I was surprised in preparing this book how often questions of religious belief came up: some of the people I talked to rejected traditional religion, others were trying to find their place within it, but in either case there seemed to be an ongoing search for spiritual self-definition. I asked Dr. John Scott, a gay Presbyterian minister, to talk about what he sees as the place for religion in gay and lesbian lives, and the place for gays and lesbians within religion.

I was very active in my local church as a teenager. I loved the youth activities, and the church youth group was in many ways my prime social group. I attended a Methodist church. And it was a church of a pretty conservative stripe, more conservative than most Methodists. I don't know that homosexuality was ever mentioned — I think it was beyond anyone's dreams that a good Methodist child might even consider be-

"I think it was beyond anyone's dreams that a good Methodist child might even consider being homosexual."

ing homosexual. And it was not in my mind, either. My discovery of myself as a gay person was really later in life, as an adult. There was a lot about the church that I really questioned and argued with and disagreed with at that point in time, too.

When I was about twenty-one or twenty-two years old, I joined the Presbyterian Church, because I had become troubled by some of the Methodist Church's very pietistic and, to me, judgmental attitudes. This was in the 1960s, a time when our whole country was concerned with civil rights and questioning authority and the rising protest against the Vietnam War. At that time, I saw a lot of Presbyterian churches and leaders being active in the very causes I felt sympathetic with, so that was part of my decision to make a change.

As I matured and began to recognize and identify recurring feelings and interests I had over a period of years, I began to question a lot of things about myself, and my sexuality was one of them. It was several years after I joined the ministry and was married and had children that I really began to question this as a serious concern.

I made the shift with pain and struggle. First there was a lot of inner questioning and talking to myself, and doing some reading about sexuality. It was a time when the gay liberation movement was becoming much more public, and there was a lot in the papers, and so in some ways it was easy to get information. And my church life was also part of the scene in my exploration because the church in which I was involved was very actively trying to be helpful to gays and lesbians in getting their own due rights in our society. It was in Fort Wayne, Indiana. The congregation where I worked was instrumental in doing public forums and being very supportive of the gay and lesbian community. I was an active part of that process, and I think more than I realized at that time had a personal investment in those issues. As I met other gay and lesbian people, things within me sort of clicked and said to me, "Gee, this is a big part of who you are, too." For quite a while I thought of myself as a primarily heterosexual person who had some homosexual sensibilities or tendencies, but gradually I allowed myself to acknowledge the strength and the frequency of my gay imagination and my thoughts and my interests in really being intimate with a man. It was very threatening, but it was something I could not set aside. It was a crisis for my personal identity, and for my sense of being a good husband to a woman whom I certainly loved and was very close to, and to my children, for whom I wanted to be a good father. It was pretty hard to imagine being gay and being a good father. And the professional risks of being self-affirming as a gay person and having any career at all in the church were very frightening.

My two girls were in their early teens at the time of the divorce. Both of them immediately let me know that they didn't think any less of me because I was gay and that they were sympathetic with what a terrible struggle and challenge it was to deal with my sexuality when I was otherwise happily married. I think my girls had a lot of maturity at that point and still do — they're both in college now. Part of it was that my wife and I had gay and lesbian friends, and so the girls had been aware of homosexuality as something that we felt fine about long before this particular crisis hit our family. It wasn't so much a matter of my being gay that was upsetting — it was the disruption of the family that was the painful thing. It was a very painful time, and yet my crisis over sexuality in some ways became a new subject for us to become closer about.

I certainly had some level of feeling guilty about being gay — some of my first thoughts were "I shouldn't let this happen to me; I'm a bad person if I allow myself to even think about being gay." That's sort of a process I worked through, though, as I realized that I wasn't *trying* to be gay. I started to think, Well, maybe these feelings really are natural, and that it's not a matter of suppressing or denying them but of figuring out how to live with them in some responsible way. I never really felt that God hated me because I had these feelings. Fairly early on I had some core belief that I wouldn't be feeling these things if they weren't natural, and if they're natural, they must somehow be part of God's plan, if indeed God plans life to that level of detail. That's certainly the way I've come to feel now, that homosexual feelings or identity per se have no moral value either way. It's no better or worse to be gay or straight. If one wants to talk about morality, we can talk about the way we *use* any part of our being to help the world or hurt the world, but being gay or being straight really has no moral quality per se.

It was a challenging time. When I became divorced, I didn't come out to my congregation and say, "I'm getting divorced because I'm gay." The process of coming out to my church was a very slow and careful process. I came out to a person at a time as I trusted them or as I thought it would be helpful for them to know that about me. Eventually I did come out to my whole congregation. I first spoke to the board of my church at a meeting one night and said that my own personal lifestyle was becoming gradually more open and I wanted to tell them before they began to hear it from someone else that I was becoming a more gay-identified person. It was scary. I had been in this particular church for about eight years, and they had hired me as a married man. I'd gone through quite a change. The divorce itself was a painful thing for the congregation, although they were very supportive of both me and my wife and people were not judgmental or gossipy or prying at the time of the divorce. That was a pretty good clue that this was a group of people that were more loving than judging. The congregation itself had lots of single people, divorced people, married people, and some gay people. It was a church that valued a diversity of lifestyles. Finally one Sunday, during the last year that I was there, I gave a sermon about what it's like to be a pastor and a gay person and about what the congregation can do to support people who are going through major life discoveries and changes and crises, and just offered myself as one example. And the response was very good.

I knew there was some potential that some Presbyterian from another church nearby might get wind of the fact that I was speaking openly about being gay and, knowing that this was in conflict with denominational standards, might make a complaint to a higher authority in the church. That certainly was a possibility and it still is a possibility, as far as that goes. I continue to hold my ordination and membership in a regional body of the Presbyterian Church, and there definitely continues to be this risk that someone may complain that I am in violation of the standards for ordination. There's a rule that has been on the books since 1978, at which time it was voted by our national General Assembly that self-affirming, practicing homosexuals are not qualified for ordination to office in the church, whether that's to be an elder or a dea-

John and his lover, Frank, in front of the church where John
served as pastor until recently

searching, and some of the traditional rituals and activities of religion such as prayer, or singing, or meditation, take on new meaning. They're new resources for living at a time when life has become more precious because it's limited. Another major issue for people living with AIDS is anger and frustration about losing life or losing one's abilities or vitality. If you look at the Judeo-Christian traditions, that's quite consistent with saints and other people down through the years who have suffered and who have often responded with anger and arguing with God. Why is this happening? Demanding a reason, demanding God to be accountable. I find it very exciting that in some ways AIDS makes life more valuable, and makes the vulnerability and the brevity of our lives, whether we have AIDS or not, seem all that much more apparent. People with terminal illnesses, whether it's AIDS or something else, often come to the conclusion that they don't want to waste their time doing things that are not rewarding or have no point, but they want to live in a way that's very much serving them and serving the world, here and now, not later. There's something very exciting and good about that in spite of the terror of the illness itself.

Of course, there are many gay and lesbian people who simply have no use for the church whatsoever; in fact the church has been one of the primary enemies against gay and lesbian well-being. I can appreciate that; it's not my task in life to convince all people that they should be part of the church. But even with all its faults and with all its history of prejudice and oppression against gays and lesbians, in fact in many, many cases religious groups have also been very helpful to gays and lesbians and have been places where self-discovery is encouraged. Within most churches there are subgroups that are very vocally and concretely supportive of gays and lesbians. It's often not admitted openly, but gays and lesbians have been the leaders in many denominations for a long time.

For those young people who feel like they have some personal connection to God and have longings for faith and for involvement in a church, I think if they will look around and be patient, they'll find that there are in fact some congregations that can be very supportive and help them. It might be a hard search, depending on where you are, but if one is a religious person, it's definitely worth it — it's an exercise in your own growth to try to find your place in a religious community. It may not be the religious community you were born into or what your family has raised you in. It may not be possible to stay in that particular religious group and get affirmation. But I think at the core, or at all people's core, is some spiritual awareness, and to ignore that part of oneself if you're sensitive to it would be tragic. If you knew you had a gift, and were afraid to use it, it would be like ignoring your gift in athletics or at writing poetry or in doing a lot of other things. Being gay is a gift. It's not the only gift, it may not be the most important gift, but it's one of the gifts of life.

RECOMMENDED FURTHER READING

Fiction

Bauer, Marion Dane, editor. *Am I Blue? Coming Out from the Silence.* New York: HarperCollins, 1994. Sixteen short stories by popular young adult authors such as M. E. Kerr, Jane Yolen, and William Sleator explore gay themes in the lives of teen protagonists.

Block, Francesca Lia. *Weetzie Bat.* New York: HarperCollins, 1989. Weetzie Bat lives in a land of glitz where she hangs out with her gay best buddy, Dirk. Her young punk life isn't quite perfect, so she makes three wishes, and they all come true.

Brett, Catherine. *S.P. Likes A.D.* Brooklyn: The Women's Press, 1990. In this simply written novel about a girl's first realization that she may be a lesbian, ninth-grader Stephanie finds herself attracted to classmate Anne.

Brown, Rita Mae. *Rubyfruit Jungle.* New York: Bantam, 1988. Brash, bawdy, and smart-mouthed Molly takes on the world in this uninhibited lesbian classic.

Garden, Nancy. *Annie on My Mind.* New York: Farrar, Straus & Giroux, 1982. Annie and Liza meet as high school students at Foster Academy, where they begin a journey into a love that they never before dreamed possible.

M. E. Kerr. *Deliver Us from Evie.* New York: HarperCollins, 1994. Evie's farm family has always accepted her butch ways as a part of her inspired self-confidence, but when Evie gets involved with the beautiful Patsy Duff, they don't know what to think — or do.

————. *Night Kites.* New York: HarperCollins, 1986. Erick, seventeen, learns about prejudice and family bonds when his gay older brother Pete, stricken with AIDS, moves back home.

Koertge, Ron. *The Arizona Kid.* Boston: Little, Brown, 1988. Sixteen-year-old Billy doesn't know what to expect when he goes off to spend a summer with his gay uncle out in the wild and woolly contemporary West.

Mullins, Hilary. *The Cat Came Back.* Tallahassee: Naiad Press, 1993. Told through seventeen-year-old Stevie Roughgarden's journal entries, this vivid story of how she arrives at accepting herself chronicles her relationships with teachers, friends, and a new classmate named Andrea.

Stadler, Matthew. *Landscape: Memory.* New York: NAL/Dutton, 1991. Set in 1914, this novel takes place in San Francisco and charts the years of a boy's passage to manhood. As memory and reality entwine, we experience Maxwell and Duncan's discovering the soul-shaking feelings of first love and romance.

Walker, Kate. *Peter.* Boston: Houghton Mifflin, 1993. In this novel from Australia, fifteen-year-old Peter is intrigued with his big brother Vince's friend David, who is self-assured, good-looking — and gay.

Nonfiction

Alyson, Sasha, editor. *Young, Gay & Proud.* Boston: Alyson Publications, 1991. For those who are young and facing their feelings of being gay or lesbian, this book answers such questions as: Am I the only one? What would my friends think if I told them? Should I tell my parents?

Cohen, Susan and Daniel. *When Someone You Know Is Gay.* New York: M. Evans, 1989. A comprehensive, easy-to-read overview of what it means to be gay.

Heron, Ann, editor. *Two Teenagers in Twenty.* Boston: Alyson Publications, 1994. In this expanded edition of *One Teenager in Ten,* young people tell their own stories in their own voices. They speak eloquently to the issues of being a gay or lesbian youth: discovering their gay feelings, deciding whether or not to tell friends and family, and coming to terms with being different.

Kuklin, Susan. *Fighting Back: What Some People Are Doing about the AIDS Crisis.* New York: Putnam, 1989. Photojournalist Susan Kuklin spent nine months volunteering with New York's Gay Men's Health Crisis organization, hearing the courageous stories of people living with AIDS.

Marcus, Eric. *Is It a Choice?* New York: HarperCollins, 1993. In this honest, compassionate, and comprehensive resource, the author answers three hundred of the most frequently asked questions about gays and lesbians. Topics include self-discovery, coming out, family and children, work, dating, and much more.

Miller, Neil. *In Search of Gay America.* New York: HarperCollins, 1989. This is a unique account of gay America through one man's eyes. Neil Miller spent the last part of the 1980s journeying through small towns, farm country, suburbs, and cities in search of the diversity of gay and lesbian life.

Steffan, Joseph. *Honor Bound: A Gay Naval Midshipman Fights to Serve His Country.* New York: Villard, 1992. Forced to resign from the U.S. Naval Academy at Annapolis after acknowledging his homosexuality, Joe Steffan decided to fight back.

— *compiled with the assistance of People Like Us Books, Chicago*

RESOURCES

Gay, Lesbian, and Bisexual
  Veterans Association
  (GLBVA)
P.O. Box 2051
Ann Arbor, MI 48106-2051

Horizons Youth Services
961 West Montana
Chicago, IL 60614
(312) 929-HELP
TDD: (312) 327-4357

National AIDS Hotline
Centers for Disease Control
(800) 342-AIDS
Spanish: (800) 344-7432
TDD: (800) 243-7889

National Gay and Lesbian
  Task Force
1734 Fourteenth St. NW
Washington, DC 20009
(202) 332-6483
TDD: (202) 332-6219

Parents, Families and Friends of
  Lesbians and Gays (P-FLAG)
1101 Fourteenth St. NW, 10th fl.
Washington, DC 20005
(202) 638-4200

For *You Are Not Alone*, a state-by-
state directory of organizations serving gay youth, send five dollars to:

> Hetrick-Martin Institute
> Public Information Department
> 2 Astor Place
> New York, NY 10003

ROGER SUTTON is editor in chief of the *Horn Book Magazine*. He is a well-known critic and teacher in the field of children's books and formerly worked as a children's and young adult librarian. As he says in the introduction to this book, he set out to create a work of nonfiction that would "show teenage gays and lesbians that life goes on past junior-high humiliation and high-school ostracism" and that would give teens a sense of gays and lesbians as a community, "united in history, culture, political goals, and perpetual disagreement." He lives in Boston.

LISA EBRIGHT has been working as a professional photographer for more than twenty years. She has done many kinds of photography, including portraiture, theatrical photography, documentary work, and fine art photography. Her work has appeared in books, magazines, and newspapers, including *Newsweek,* the *Advocate, Personal Property,* and the *Chicago Tribune.* She lives in Chicago.

$8.95   FPT

$11.95 in Canada

Praise for
HEARING US OUT

"A moving and humanizing look at a particular experience....Sutton breaks down stereotypes and gives human faces to a topic that needs yet greater visibility in young-adult literature."   — *Horn Book*

"Young and old — from teenager to grandmother — give a sharp taste of what it is like to be gay in America."   — *Kirkus*

"This lively title both demystifies a minority group demonized by much of the media and shows teens that there is 'something to look forward to' in spite of the discrimination and loneliness they feel."
   — *School Library Journal*

"We learn so much from simply listening to each other, and the rich, personal stories in *Hearing Us Out* have much to teach us."   — *Mitzi Henderson, President*
Parents, Families and Friends of Lesbians and Gays
(P-FLAG)

"*Hearing Us Out* is a moving book that stands as an important addition for those interested in learning more about the lives of lesbians and gay men. It will be especially welcomed by young people coming out in today's world in search of diverse role models as well as guidance on how to survive and thrive."
   — *Frances Kunreuther, Executive Director*
The Hetrick-Martin Institute

"This is a splendid and empowering book, which I hope will reach many, many young people."   — *Nancy Garden, author of* Annie on My Mind

An ALA Best Book for Young Adults

A *Hungry Mind Review*
Children's Book of Distinction

10970870
Printed in the U.S.A.

ISBN 0-316-82313-9

90000

EAN

9 780316 823135